Bannana's Near Death Experiences

Ode to Steve Jobs

Martti Vallila

Copyright © 2015 Martti Vallila

All rights reserved.

ISBN: 1492161810
ISBN-13: 9781492161813

Martti Vallila

FOR ROSE
AND HER GREAT-GRANDCHILDREN
HERE THEY LEARN ABOUT
GRANDPA

For Marja,
My first companion
on this journey.

Love,
Martti
5/29/2016

Bannana's Near Death Experiences

Table of Contents

Answering Steve Jobs' challenge	page 4
Early childhood	page 11
Skiing on snow and water	page 17
Community organizing in Alabama	page 43
Stanford and exploring California	page 51
French medicine	page 62
Impressions of Japan	page 71
The islands and jungles of the Philippines	page 77
Islamic teachings	page 217
The south side of Chicago	page 221
Passing through New York	page 232
Russia, my muse	page 237
Fleeing Finland	page 241
Rose, the pioneer	page 251
Boston, my final resting place	page 253

Answering Steve Jobs' challenge

I have lived much of my life as a near death experience, on the edge. All of life is, in fact, a near death experience, as Steve Jobs pointed out in his seminal address to Stanford graduates in 2005, perhaps the most profound 12 minutes available on You Tube. Live life as if each day is your last was one of the messages succinctly conveyed by Jobs in that address, made shortly after he knew his days on earth were numbered. Another message from that talk was that the decisions you make are understandable only when looking back, when "connecting the dots".

Decisions, at the time they are made, are informed by an unconscious instinct or calling. Do not be afraid to follow your impulses, advised Jobs. You probably won't understand why your instincts are telling you something. Just go for it! It will make sense later. The example Steve used in that speech was his inexplicable interest in calligraphy while at Reed which became important later when he insisted that his first computer be capable of reproducing the world's best collection of fonts. This passion with the quality of its available fonts provided Apple its initial foothold in publishing.

As I listened, for the first time, to that speech on You Tube in 2012, at age 63, I reflected that I had done a fairly good job of following his advice before having gotten it. I realized that my mother Rose had infused me with confidence and a sense of adventure that led me to follow a path that probably would have met with his approval. I certainly do not (yet) have his wealth as a result but I am blessed with something more important: confidence that I have lived life on my own terms, and that, given the chance to do it over, I would make the same choices. As Edith Piaf, who Rose enjoyed listening to, immortalized, "je ne regrette rien".

In 2005 Jobs was giving advice to the graduating class of one of the most prestigious (and expensive) universities in the world, telling them to follow their "inner calling" to the degree they recognized one, challenging them to look! I did not find my calling until I was close to forty. Until that time I was in preparation. After discovering Asia, thanks to a teaching job on the southern Philippine Island of Mindanao, I worked for three years on the railroad in America, first in DC, then Seattle and finally in Chicago where I took a serious job with IBM (while getting an MBA at night from the University of Chicago), as my life took a serious turn. I got married and had two daughters in Chicago. Big blue took us from there to New York, then Paris, and finally to North Carolina during my 15-year carrier.

All that was, in retrospect, preparation for a calling that awaited me. That calling emerged when, in 1991, the Soviet Union collapsed. Having been born on one side of the Iron Curtain, in Czechoslovakia, and educated on the other, in business, I felt I had a responsibility to do something at what I recognized as a key geopolitical moment in East-West relations. What led me to this decision, to jump into the story of a "new Russia", is told in my first book "Bannana in Russia; Commercializing Transformational Technologies".

Difficulties I subsequently faced are described in my second book, "Bannana in the Legal Gulag; Exposing Trickery and Manipulation" and my third, "Bannana's Crime and Punishment; 'Justice in Finland". As Steve explains in his video he learned more from failure, when he was fired from the company he founded, than from any of his successes. I have been convicted, in Finland, of the crime of "aggravated embezzlement" for attempting to bring a promising treatment of Alzheimer's to the country by forming a company Buddha Biopharma Oy there and requesting the funding support of the government. Problems in Finland led me to found my future companies in Singapore.

Following my firing from my position as Managing Director of Buddha Biopharma (for the crime of having paid myself a salary), the company moved its work from Finland to Kazakhstan, where clinical trials took place in secret. The results of those trials will one day emerge and deliver to the world the treatment it desperately awaits. That story will be told in other "Bannana books". (My choice of Bannana as a nom de plume is fully explained at the start of "Bannana in Russia". The short explanation: Vallila, when written in Cyrillic, resembles "Bannina".)

***

The inspiration for this book was the death of my mother, Rose. When I entered the Georgetown house she lived her last days in, on N Street, I discovered, among the papers in the top drawer of a dresser next to her bed, signs of a book she had started, telling the story of her escape from Czechoslovakia, where I was born, to America where we moved when I was seven. Rose's book did not have many pages. It was enough for me to know that she wanted to write one. What a book it would have been!

It would have spoken of an early childhood in a well-to-do coal mining family, marriage at a young age to a young man from a good family with whom she had a boy who died from infection after the bite of an insect in post-war Prague. That shock inspired a divorce, and subsequent marriage to a handsome Finnish diplomat, Olli Vallila, sixteen years older, who took her from Prague to Geneva, where he was Finland's representative to the original GATT talks, and then to Belgrade from where their paths diverged. Rose left for America and Olli went back to Finland. In America Rose settled in Georgetown and became one of the best known, and well-respected agents of her day.

She was well known to my friends many of who considered her a wise aunt, if not a second mother, for the "old world wisdom" she provided them, often over scotch, during late evening conversations she hosted with European flair. Her wisest investments were houses she bought and resold, after renovating them with my help. After I left DC for college in California our time together was restricted to my visits "home", first alone and then, after a visit during which I met my future wife Dominique, with our two daughters who we were happy to leave in Rose's loving care when they were too young to join us for skiing. I spoke often to Rose about writing a book. Not as often as I asked her to stop smoking!

Unlike the second request, which was impossible, given the habit Rose had cultivated all her life (and that would kill her), writing a book seemed like something that could occupy her time and challenge her intellect. But it was not to be. Except for a handful of pages, typed on yellowing paper, with notes in pencil in the margins in handwriting I recognized as hers....evidence of a start...

The second discovery I made in the dresser, enclosed in a transparent folder, were typed copies of letters I had sent her from the Philippines! She had lovingly transcribed her understanding of my early hand-written prose, sent during a time when I was travelling in the Asian jungle, encountering many near death experiences, and casually referencing pirates and shark-infested waters. Deciding to participate in Stanford's "Volunteers in Asia" program was a spur of the moment decision (one of those Steve Jobs "dots") that satisfied my need to have a first-hand experience in Asia, without a gun in my hand, and a chance to try teaching in a context that could be considered "fieldwork".

Here were letters offering a precious window into my youth. What a glorious surprise. A sudden communication from the past! I recognized them for what they were: a loving tribute to a son gone far away, of who she was proud. They followed me from North Carolina (where I was living when Rose passed) to San Francisco, Paris, Chicago, back to San Francisco and then Boston, as my possessions dwindled and my life simplified. How might they become relevant?

In Boston I wrote three books. Why not base a fourth around these letters, a book on the more general theme of "near death experiences", of the financial, as well as the physical kind? World events were pointing to a need for such a book. Radical Islam is on the march, worldwide. The Boston Marathon bombing created awareness in my new hometown. Discussions of Islam are likely to increase feeding, perhaps, interest in first-hand accounts, and reflections informed by them.

    Thoughts about Islam are relevant to another area of my activity, my attempt to bring Russia and the West closer together. (How's that for a "near death experience"?) My answer is through collaboration in the actualization (commercialization) of technology. A project more likely to bring Russia and the West together is the common need to fight radical Islamic terror.

    Russia, survivor of the Soviet Union, is caught in its own identity struggle. How to leave a resource-dependent past and step into a connected future? The benefits of integrating with the West must be made real. Technologies that are making the world "flat" (in Tom Friedman's terms) exist and will become more pervasive, powerful enough to envelop even this largest of countries, although, as I joke with my Russian friends, for something so inevitable, it sure is taking its time...

    The "stability" of mutually assured destruction has been replaced by a new terror illustrated by the Boston bombing, attacks on innocents in Paris, and numerous other cold-blooded killing driven by a religion I first experienced in Mindanao in 1971. I have no idea how this new struggle against Jihadist terror will end. I am not confident about the West's ability to prevail, given its absurd reluctance to call it what it is. A contribution I *can* make to this existential struggle of civilizations is to share personal experiences from a time long ago and a place far away.

***

    The Philippines have been, historically, a battleground of religions. The first religious beliefs were the animist beliefs of the natives, probably as diverse as the languages spoken on the thousands of islands that today form the country.

When external religions projected their influence, the Philippine Islands found them-selves at the frontier of conflict. Christianity came along with Magellan, in 1521. The first man to circumnavigate the globe died in Cebu, killed by the native leader Lapu-Lapu. Christianity conquered the islands with assistance from Spain. Later, during a period of worldwide expansion on the part of Islam, with Spain herself under Moorish influence, Islam met Christianity in the Philippines.

Islam displayed an ability to integrate itself into local culture, finding its place into "lalang" the "high language" recited by elders that is the fabric of the Maranao world. Moslems provided the fiercest resistance to both Japanese and Americans during World War II. Today they occupy only the interior high ground of the enormous southern island of Mindanao and the islands of the Sulu Archipelago that point from Mindanao in the direction of Indonesia (the nation with the world's largest Moslem population).

Those precious letters provided a pretext for starting a book that would be a context for observations about two areas that both have a chance to contribute to a rapprochement between East and West: commercializing technology and fighting terror. I needed an overall theme.

Sometimes when among friends, or when I meet an interesting person, I ask them if they have had any "near death experiences". This often *does* lead to memorable conversations. Biking across the Charles on the day I reviewed the digital version of "Bannana in the Legal Gulag" on my daughter Sofia's Mac, and after having a "near death" experience dodging a car on Mass Ave, the title of this book came to me like a bolt. I would write a book about "near death experiences" of both the financial and physical sort.

My time in the Philippines had provided plenty of brushes with physical death. I had been brought near to financial death several times in San Francisco, after buying the house whose roof I am standing on in the cover photo at the time I was leaving IBM, confident that things would work out. And in Finland, where my attempts to form a company there to commercialize a promising treatment for Alzheimer's has resulted in my conviction as an "embezzler".

Things have indeed worked out (I am still alive) but not in a way I could have imagined. As Jobs said, connecting dots is only possible looking back...

Early childhood

As far as I know my birth in Prague, Czechoslovakia, in 1949 was without complications. I was born not in a hospital, but in a third-floor apartment inhabited by my Finnish diplomatic father, Olli and his Czech bride, sixteen years younger, Ruzena, who was twenty-five at the time. I was shown the place years later by an uncle, who took me to the building. People occupying the first floor confirmed that a diplomatic family had lived there after the war. The current tenants were not home so I was allowed inside (they had a key). There was one sunlit room, next to the master bedroom, that seemed the obvious place for a baby.

At age fifty-five I finally saw my birthplace. Neither of my parents had any reason to return to Prague, once the family left in 1952 for Geneva, my father's next diplomatic post. I did have an early illness, difficulty breathing, for which I was given penicillin, to which I am told I had a reaction that almost killed me, but I do not remember this.

The first ailment I remember was a revulsion to boiled eggs that developed because I loved them so much that, one day I ate so many that it made me sick. I vomited what I had eaten, on a beach in Torremolinos, Spain, and it took more than twenty years before I could stomach the yellow of an egg again. I couldn't stand the smell of boiled eggs for years. I started eating egg whites years earlier, and now enjoy easy-over eggs, but it took years to get over my trauma.

That doesn't qualify as a "near death experience", but it does demonstrate the ability of the human body first to create a phobia and then be healed of it, over time. The first serious physical trauma I remember was slipping on the ice outside the English speaking Catholic school I attended in Helsinki, during the only winter we lived in Finland. The fall caused a bloody wound over my right eyebrow that I infected by pulling a woolen car over the spot to stop the bleeding. A scar, partially hidden by an eyebrow, marks the spot to this day.

A vicarious near death experience was suffered that winter by our neighbor Sakkari, who was walking on the ice just beyond the wooden pier outside Marjukkala, the log house on the water just outside of Helsinki that my parents had built soon after their marriage. The ice was thin and collapsed under him. Fortunately his upper body remained above the ice and he was able to work his way to the pier, and safety.

Most of my Marjukkala memories are summer moments, fishing off the pier, collecting blueberries on the hill behind the house, searching for mushrooms in the surrounding forest. We were living that winter in Marjukkala while Rose looked for an apartment in Helsinki. That was my only winter in Finland. That winter I skied for the first time on the frozen water. I remember cross-country skiing in near darkness through parks where the trails were marked with color spots on the trees. I remember playing hockey on a portion of ice cleared of snow, rippled by wind, and sometimes losing a puck when it disappeared into the water through an opening.

There is not much light in Finland in the winter. I recall waking up in Marjukkala, walking through the woods to the bus stop, taking the bus to downtown Helsinki, switching to a tram that took me to the Catholic school, and the sun rising shortly after I got there. The trip home was also made in darkness. Time on the playground, when there was light, was precious. It was during one of those midday frolics outdoors that I slipped and fell, cracking my head open. We finally moved into an apartment in town not far from the school making the daily commute a snap. The danger was the coat of ice covering the playground equipment where I would skate in the dark. I was told not to lick such ice in search of refreshment, warned that my tongue would stick to the ice and would have to be ripped off. I never dared challenge this warning with an experiment.

I remember accompanying my father to a ski jumping competition in Lahti on a bus that was so full of smokers that it formed revulsion to cigarette smoke that stayed with me for years. The revulsion was not overcome by social pressure when I was offered a cigarette years later, in the bushes at Montrose Park. I took a drag and found the experience so unpleasant that I couldn't imagine why it was considered such a big deal. That revulsion has lasted a lifetime.

Much of my socialization into American society occurred on Georgetown playground. I was lucky that the playground employed a full time recreational director, George Todd. George was as much of a father figure as I had in America. I learned baseball and American football on his playground. I also learned to defend myself, with words, and sometimes with fists. When I first showed up to play baseball my new teammates suggest I catch but didn't mention that a mask was as much a part of the uniform as a big, round glove. They were curious to see if I would get behind the plate without one. Knowing no better, I agreed.

I watched a lot of baseball on black and white TV to learn the rules as well as the English language. As a member of the boy patrol I received a ticket to a Washington Senators game in fourth grade as a gift. I will never forget my first visit to Griffith Stadium, and the moment I understood for the first time the scale at which the game was played, how lush the outfield was, how immense a major league field was!

I learned to enjoy the catcher position. My first pitcher was Dawson Wan, a Chinese boy who matured much faster than the rest of us. As a consequence Dawson was the pitcher on our 12-and-under team. He could throw very fast. The problem was that Dawson had little control over where his pitches would go. I had problems catching some of his pitches but my main concern was getting the ball back to Dawson without embarrassing myself. I did not have a very accurate arm myself. Throwing a runner out at second or third was something I was unlikely to do. I focused on keeping my throws to Dawson from bouncing on the ground so as not to invite too many challenges from base runners.

    Dawson contributed to my biggest baseball accident, not with a fast pitch but a very slow, underhand throw. There was a runner at third and the batter hit a dribbler in Dawson's direction. I signaled that he should throw the ball to first. Instead, Dawson underhanded a ball that took forever to get to me. It arrived at about the same instant as the runner from third who knocked me cold when he and I collided. I held onto the ball and was credited with a put out to end the inning. I was the first batter up at the top of the next inning. When I looked at the opposing pitcher my eyesight went spotty, my ability to focus was not there. I received a walk. When I got to first base I mentioned to George, who was coaching there, that I had had difficulty seeing the pitcher's head, much less the balls he was throwing. Hearing this George took me out and called an ambulance. That was my first ambulance ride. X-rays were negative.

    Another memorable childhood accident occurred on the soccer field. I played goalie. In a game on a rainy day an opponent kicked me in the mouth, causing the loss of a tooth. I was taken into the first aid room where I was soon joined by the guy who had kicked me in an act of retaliation on the part of my teammates. I took this as the sign of solidarity it was meant to be. We played touch football against teams from neighboring playgrounds. I was fast and could catch, so my position was flanker on offense, with Dawson as my quarterback, defensive back on defense. Our most effective offensive play, which we saved for key moments, was a delay over the middle by the flanker (me) after all other receivers had led the defense in the opposite direction.

    Our deceptive tactics usually resulted in an open target for Dawson. All he had to do was throw the football with accuracy, and slowly enough to make it catch-able. Dawson's tendency to throw everything at full speed was frustratingly impossible to correct. Dawson became very sick in his twenties, and died an early death from a mysterious illness. His life had followed its own, unique, dynamic. Early development made him a giant among twelve year olds. Those same hormones may have had something to do with robbing Dawson of older age.

When it snowed and sometimes when it didn't, some of us played tackle football, without equipment. I earned the respect of many when I displayed fearlessness, taking on larger players before understanding much about the game. I certainly didn't look for fights and was able to diffuse most situations with talk, but playground life was rough. My most memorable experiences with George Todd, the coach who taught me baseball and football, were not on the athletic field, but on the stage. George's passion was theater. There was a citywide public playground competition every winter. The first couple of years George recruited me, and my sister, into roles for plays he chose out of a catalogue.

One year George decided he was ready to produce an original version of an American classic, The Wizard of Oz. In order to develop the script George listened to a recording and transcribed the words and songs into a script. Some of the sounds were not understandable. On songs where he couldn't make out all the words George wrote down the sounds. I had never seen the movie, never even heard the story, until George explained his project and told me he wanted me to play a lion. George wanted Marja, my sister, to play the good witch. Dorothy would be played by a girl I had a crush on. I was in.

Never considered seeing the movie (among the most viewed movies of all time). Had no idea who Bert Lahr was. Several of the lion's songs did not include words but sounds, which I learned to imitate. My costume consisted of a lion outfit and a mop, died yellow. My favorite part was the opening song where I understood all of the words and could shake my tail at a dramatic moment, which always got the laugh it was intended to elicit. The tin man was played by

Norman Binstead, younger brother of Tommy (one of my biggest playground tormentors). This changed my relationship with the Binsteads, considered the kings of the playground. Full reconciliation occurred years later when I asked Tommy to introduce me when I ran for student body vice president at Western, a race I lost. (My platform consisted of running as Batman. Posters saying "Vote Vallila" in white lettering, each word on a separate wing of a black bat, were posted all over school.)

    We got to perform The Wizard of Oz three times. We won in preliminary rounds and reached the city finals. My performance in the finals won me the best actor award and remains a cherished memory of childhood. I am happy to start into the lion song at the slightest suggestion...."If I were king of the forrrrest, not queen, nor duke, nor prince..."

    I finally saw the movie in Chicago at age 25, when it played in the theater around the corner from the apartment in Lincoln Park I was occupying. I later learned that the author of the story, L. Frank Baum, lived in Lincoln Park when he wrote his classic.

Skiing on snow and water

Having learned to ski in Finland without the aid of any lifts I continued this habit in Georgetown, in the hills of Montrose Park, off Wisconsin Avenue (where I had that encounter with my first cigarette). On the infrequent days it would snow (and close the city) I would walk with wooden skis up Wisconsin Avenue and try my rusty skills on the slopes not far from Dumbarton Oaks (where the United Nations charter was signed). There was more sledding than skiing going on. Our financial situation was such that paying to ski made no sense.

I did not ride a chairlift until my first winter at Stanford when new friends introduced me to the wonders of Lake Tahoe. I rented skis at Squaw Valley and went immediately up the mountain to Shirley Lake, assuring my friends I knew how to ski. I was amazed at the improvement that being able to ride up a mountain on a lift provided to the skiing experience! Getting down the steep slopes proved more difficult than I had anticipated. That day I made many face plants, attacking the mountain with an enthusiasm that impressed my companions, all legitimately good skiers. I kept at it on the next day and by the end of the weekend I could say that I did, now, know how to ski!

I became proficient skiing on water much earlier. Once we could afford it we went for two-week vacations from DC to Provincetown, Massachusetts, on the tip of Cape Cod, a place introduced to us by friends of Rose who lived in New York. Provincetown was then a normal place (before its transformation into a homosexual mecca). The seaside cabins we occupied, in North Truro, were as close to heaven as anything I knew on earth. How I looked forward to those two weeks of summer, an escape from Washington humidity in cottages cooled by a constant sea breeze, with an enormous block of ice delivered each day for refrigeration.

On the summer of my twelfth birthday I approached a group with a ski boat staying in a house down the beach after observing their fun from a distance and asked if I could give the sport a try. They agreed, put me in a life preserver, instructing me to "stay in a ball until the boat picked up sufficient speed" and then to stand up. I followed those instructions and soon found myself, magically, above water, able to balance and maneuver the skis. I was able to make it outside the wake during that first ride that I completed without falling. I returned to shore a changed man. Rose and Marja, my younger sister, had watched with admiration. I was hooked. My new friends provided me rides each day for the remainder of our stay whenever they were there. I could think of little else the rest of the summer.

The next summer those neighbors were there (thank God) and Junior, the boat owner, explained the next step in water skiing, starting with two and dropping one ski. I gave it a try and can't say that I didn't fall on my first try, but I was able to balance on that one leg for a considerable length of time before placing it on the back of the ski, which invoked motion that threw me off. A key decision to make when moving to the slalom ski is which leg goes in front, which one goes in back. One way to address this question is to raise each leg as one is skiing on two skis to determine which one feels most comfortable as the "stable leg". Such experimentation on my part revealed a preference for my left leg. (With the authority of a waterskiing teacher that I was to become I predict that if you are right handed chances are you will prefer the left leg forward, if you are left handed the reverse is likely to be true.)

After that summer our habits changed. Rather than drive to Provincetown we vacationed in more accessible Rehoboth Beach, a two-hour drive from DC, known as "the nation's summer capital". Friends were renting a home, which we shared, and it was OK with me as long as I could water ski. There was a water skiing operation in a marina on the bay using an inboard-outboard Chris Craft boat that was superior to Junior's classic 60-horse outboard. Marja was a decent skier on two skis and willing to ski while I rested between rides, but the hour that Rose booked each day was primarily for me. The only thought I had every morning was how windy it would be at the hour we had reserved. The middle of the day was risky, late afternoon preferable. The guys running the business recognized my enthusiasm, and growing skill. There was talk that the summer of my 16th year I might be welcomed as an assistant of some sort in their business. (I was ready to do anything.)

We lived in Georgetown so the idea of owning a boat was out of the question. Until Rose saw an inflatable Zodiac in France during the trip we took to Europe the year of my 16th birthday. Rose had sold quite a few houses and was in a position to take us to Europe for the first time since we had arrived by boat in 1958. She organized a grand tour whose highlight was my 16th birthday in Paris, dinner at La Perouse, after which we all went to Le Moulin Rouge where I saw my first cancan! Marja was a willing, if somewhat embarrassed, participant in this right of passage. (She probably thought of it as a "near death experience".)

Once Rose saw Zodiacs zipping along the water, powered by 40 horsepower engines, she decided she had the perfect birthday present for me: an inflatable boat we could store in our basement, and equip with a powerful enough engine (bought used) to create a combination of sufficient speed to ski behind. Rose added a business angle. Zodiacs were unknown in the US. There might be a market for them in America. She contacted Zodiac headquarters and negotiated some arrangement that did not concern or interest me at the time. I was happy to have my Zodiac (probably purchased at a discount), shipped to America in the trunk of the car Rose had brought to Europe.

As the next summer approached we drove to Rehoboth looking for the water ski operation and received shocking news. There would be no waterskiing business that summer operating out of the marina, no summer job for me. There was another alternative. I had my Zodiac and a used 40-horse power engine. I could operate my own waterskiing business, Rose suggested. This would not be a Chris Craft operation but maybe I could fill a gap created by the unexpected news. I thought it was a great idea. We needed to find a facility on the bay (where the water was most often calm) willing to host such a business. We approached Bob Vignola, owner of Rainbow Cove Marina, once a football lineman at the University of Delaware. "Big Vig" ran the motel as his main business. The marina in the back was a side business, providing boating facilities to guests.

From my point of view the location was ideal. It was next door to the marina that had hosted the previous waterskiing operation, the long dock extended far enough into the bay that the water was deep enough at its end to ski in. A platform at the end of that dock would serve as a base for my water skiing operation. The gas facility that was part of the marina had a pay phone that could be used for reservation purposes. Rainbow Cove Motel & Marina had a huge sign on the road leading into town, under which could be added a painted notice announcing water skiing, and the phone number of the pay phone. Negotiations were brief. I offered to split my revenue with him. "Big Vig" saw any revenue as gravy in his marina cash flow. There was no discussion of insurance. I was understood to be liable for any risks although the thought never really entered my mind. "Big Vig" agreed. I was free to start my business at his place.

I found a place to sleep, in a boarding house not too far from the marina. I had a car, a red and white Metropolitan convertible, and the prospect of running my own business as a first job. In retrospect I appreciate how unlikely a venture Rose was encouraging me to pursue. Her Zodiac gift made the audacious idea possible. Her encouragement was equally important. The rest was up to me. I built a sign from four planks of wood, painted it white, filled it with black lettering announcing my services, and nailed it under the giant pink and blue welcome to the Rainbow Cove Motel road-sign and waited for customers.

My first customer was a heavyset man who had not done much, if any, skiing prior to our encounter. He expressed surprise at seeing my inflatable ski boat. Nevertheless he and his daughters jumped in. I was embarrassed when I turned the engine to full throttle and was unable to achieve sufficient speed to reach a plane and flatten out. I was sitting on the pontoon at the back of the boat, controlling the engine with my right hand. The boat was bending slightly. I asked his daughters to move further forward in order to move their weight into a place that would allow us to achieve a speed necessary to pull their father out of the water. We succeeded. Before reaching adequate speed the Zodiac did bend. The wooden sideboards that held the boat together once the pontoons were inflated with a foot-pump to adequate pressure provided only limited stiffness.

Three people in the boat trying to pull a heavy set man, not a good skier, out of the water (my first customer combination) pretty much set the limit on what was possible. Once the Zodiac achieved a plane and the nose came back down it was fast enough to pull a skier, even on a slalom ski (I could slow her down if I made a sharp turn). Before my second year of business I invested in a mechanism that allowed me to steer the boat while sitting near the front, providing much needed ballast. During that first year I was forced to steer from the back and ask observers to move to the front of the boat to strategic locations.

Zodiacs and their imitators are today well known not as ski boats, but as stable crafts for scuba diving or rescue operations, or as evacuation options on large yachts. In 1965 they were unknown in America. Some people wanting to ski left once they saw my "ski boat", an inflatable raft with an outdoor engine, but I had enough customers, at $10 an hour, to pay for my dinners and lodging and to begin putting money in the bank. On days when the wind was up I went to the Atlantic side and tried my hand at surfing.

My big break came with the arrival of the McKinney family, or clan. The clan was a combination of two large families, one from Kentucky and the other from Maryland. There were seven Kentucky kids and five in the Maryland group. All were athletic. The leader was Francis McKinney, a woman who had married two husbands, the second a jockey. Her first three children were girls, Lee, Laura, Ouisha, the fourth, Steve, a tall boy, then (from the jockey) a smaller son, McLain, and two daughters, Sheila, and Tamara. I didn't meet them all that first day when Francis arrived and told me she wanted two hours every day for the two weeks the families would be spending together.

This Kennedy-like family contained the first human destined to be clocked at over 200km an hour, in 1978 in Portillo, Chile, (Steve) and the first American woman to win the overall World Cup (Tamara in 1983). Steve was the closest to me in age. Tamara was three when we first met and she took her first waterskiing ride behind my Zodiac. (She had practiced in a swimming pool, pulled by her brothers, before receiving my instructions.) The kids all played musical instruments, rode horses, and were home schooled (by Francis) so they could ski during the winter, when they moved from Kentucky to Reno, Nevada.

As with the Kennedys, there was tragedy along with the glory with the McKinneys. At age twelve McClain was considered the best skier his age in the world in the opinion of many in South America where he participated in summer training camps along with many of the world's elite young skiers. He killed himself at fifteen. Sheila was badly injured in a skiing accident before she reached twenty and Steve died in the back of his car, in his sleep, as a truck plowed into him off Highway 5 in California. I learned of Steve's death on an airplane when opening a ski magazine and seeing an article titled "In Memory of Steve McKinney" whose first sentence was something like " for a man who risked his life in so many ways, to be killed in his sleep on the side of a highway is the greatest of ironies."

Tamara's attempts to fulfill her mother's dream of seeing one of her children win an Olympic medal were frustrated by injuries during Olympic years. Before dying of cancer Francis saw her youngest child become overall World Cup champion in 1983, the only American woman to accomplish this until Lindsey Vonn did it three times in 2008-2010. Seeing them all ski on water Rose remembers my prediction that Tamara would be the best skier of them all.

The McKinneys invited me to stay in their Reno home when they learned that I was going to Stanford and I became a member of the family. Steve showed me parts of Squaw Valley and Taos that are not only "off piste" but considered un-skiable. I learned from him that 90% of skiing is in the mind. Most of our skiing together was done on Mt. Rose, a great mountain close to their Reno house. One spring weekend Steve, Elliot (a Stanford friend of mine), and I were skiing the main lift of Mt. Rose, through trees. I had noticed someone on a ski-do, a contraption you can sit on while wearing short skis, over my shoulder as I was speeding down the hill.

A moment later I felt a thud in my head. My first thought was that the idiot on the ski-do had somehow managed to run into me. I then realized where I was, at the base of a fairly large tree. I looked down at my knee. I saw blood. I was wearing shorts so my skin was exposed. I wiped the blood off and saw another drop fall, from my head. I put a patch of snow to my head that turned instantly red. I was compressed in a small hole at the base of the tree. Steve and Elliot were further down the hill. I had no choice but to gather myself, put on my skis and continue to the base of the lift where people in line started to point in my direction as I passed.

A scalp wound breeds a lot. My wound would require twelve stitches to close when we got to Reno. The first aid cabin had only a Kotex feminine napkin that was attached to my head with bandaging that wrapped under my chin.

"You better get to Reno fast," I was advised by the ski patrol. Steve and Elliot piled into my car, which I insisted on driving. We went to the emergency room where I was placed on a cot and covered with a white sheet, allowing access only to the portion of my head requiring immediate attention. I was asked my age and when I answered that I was seventeen the nurse asked me for a phone number of a next of kin who was an adult. I gave them Rose's number in Washington DC.

Her Saturday afternoon was interrupted by a call from the emergency room of the Reno hospital, requesting permission to sew up her son's head. Her only question:

"Are his brains OK?"

She was told I was joking with the staff, and with Steve, who described the area of my head, now shaved, as resembling open lips. The operation was a success and we went out to dinner after which I thought it would be a good idea to phone Rose who answered after one ring. I assured her that I was all right and would take it easy on the slopes on Sunday, which I did.

Steve and I were going to write a book together, my proposed title : "Zen Skiing", its content consisting of the conversations we would have while skiing various mountains. Steve learned there was a calm, a stillness, in speed. The less he did, the faster he skied.

One day, while living in Chicago, I noticed a small article in the sports section of the Tribune headlined: American sets land speed record. I had a hunch I knew who it was. Sure enough, it was Steve. With a body too big for slalom Steve became the world champion of speed. He told me later of how he and a friend had gone early to Italy, to the Kilometro Lanciato ("flying kilometer") where the time trials would be held. They camped in the surrounding mountains, taking in "the spirit" of the area. The snows came and then the national teams arrived, with their trucks of equipment and support staff.

When the time trials started Steve had the fastest times. As the elevation of the starting point increased competitors dropped out. Steve borrowed world-class equipment from other racers. He set his world record wearing the neoprene suite and helmet borrowed from a Finn about his size. He held the world speed record for five years and became the first man to hand glide off Mt. Everest. I can think of no man I know who faced more "near death experiences" then Steve McKinney. This giant of a man met his end in his sleep.

The last time we skied together was at Alpine Meadows one spring when the US team was training there. As Steve and I were riding up a lift together he shouted to a skier below who launched a huge snowball in our direction, with dangerous accuracy and speed. It was Tommy Moe, future Olympic champion. Years later skiing at Mt. Rose I met an old timer who remembered Steve as the strongest man he ever knew. When you touched his body all you felt was muscle, like steel, he recalled.

I had a few "near death experiences" trying to follow Steve down mountains. One I share here was at Taos, one of my favorites. I was wearing a knit cap with my name on it, a gift from Steve's sister Ouisha who knitted them as a business. Steve took me to the backside of the mountain where I did a somersault in the middle of which that cap was removed from my head. I searched for it for some time before giving up. Given how remote the area we were skiing was, the cap may still be there... Steve taught me to ski fresh powder in the backcountry, a habit that got me into some trouble.

Probably the day I got closest to dying on a mountain was my first day skiing on Mt. Pilchuck, a small rugged mountain not far from Seattle where I was living at the time. I had heard about the mountain from Beth, my girlfriend at Stanford, and decided to have a look one Saturday. As I approached the resort a deer ran across the road. I swerved trying to avoid it, but could not. The young deer's head hit my front bumper. It was dead. I figured that I had just been given, by fate, all the deer meat I could eat. After putting a plastic bag over the bleeding head I was able to load the animal into the forward trunk of the Volkswagen I was driving, and continued on my way.

It was still snowing when I reached the mountain. I bought my ticket and took the lift to the top, figuring there would be lots of fresh powder between the trees. There was fog. I paid no attention to the trail, tracked out by skiers, and headed in a direction promising fresh snow. Visibility was poor. I continued my traverse and soon found myself on a slippery, steep slope. I tried to catch the branches of the surrounding trees but they were too small to hang onto and bent, letting me continue to slip. I was soon in a free fall the length of which I could not imagine, off a mountain I did not know. I instinctively protected my head with my arms. In moments I felt a thud. I had landed, safely, in snow. Above me I saw a wall of rock perhaps a hundred feet high.

One ski was near me, the other hopelessly lost. I had my poles, attached to my wrists. All appendages appeared in good shape. I had no idea where I was, only knew that I could not stay there. I put my one ski on, felt the adrenalin flowing, and started a trek on one ski in a direction I hoped would lead to civilization. After about fifteen minutes I noticed some telephone wires, then a chair lift. I emerged from the woods exhausted, needing immediate rest.

"So you're the guy who fell off the onion! People have been out looking for you. We could see the tracks. You sure are lucky, buddy, that there was lots of snow where you landed."

The ski patrol showed me a black and white photo on the wall of the sheet of rock I had fallen off of. I will never forget the sensation I felt at the start of that fall, not having any idea of how long it would be, whether I would be alive when it ended. I fell into a deep sleep that lasted a couple of hours before gaining the strength to drive back to Seattle. I got to town about 10 and called my friend Scott, telling him I had a deer that needed skinning. Could he help? He arrived with a big knife and we took the carcass to a tree in a park near my apartment, hung the young female upside down and opened up her steaming interior by the light of a full moon. Did not want to think about what a passerby might think the two of us were doing. No one stopped or said anything. I learned later that what I had done was illegal. Can't recall now what laws I had violated.

I had gutted fish but never a mammal. Seeing the guts spill out and feeling the warmth of the body was an almost sexual experience. I offered Scott as much meat as he wanted and took the rest home. It filled the freezer. What didn't fit I threw out. I had deer meat omelets for breakfast, and deer meat stir-fry for dinner for quite some time, and friends were offered deer meat steaks.

My sales territory with Amtrak in Seattle consisted of British Columbia, Idaho and Montana (I had volunteered to take this geography off the hands of the more experienced members of the staff appreciating the mountains contained within.) I was able to combine visits to travel agents, my official job, with an exploration of the surrounding ski resorts, thereby enlarging my understanding of why people might want to take the train to places like Whitefish Montana, Sandpoint Idaho and Vancouver, Canada. I visited Whistler Mountain when there were practically no places there to stay overnight. (Subsequent development brought the 2010 Olympic games to these spectacular mountains, which, thankfully, will never change.)

In 1973 it was possible to overnight in bunk beds at lodges catering to ski bums. Most skiers drove from nearby Vancouver skied the day and returned home. Blackcomb Mountain has now been developed and the place has transformed into a skier's destination mecca. As one looks north one sees enough virgin mountain ranges to swallow all the world's skiers, I was once told by a local. Access to them is limited to those who heli-ski in for wilderness adventures.

My heli-skiing memory is limited to a one-day chance made available to me when Dominique and I were visiting a recently opened mountain at the very eastern edge of British Columbia, just over the boarder from Alberta. We had flown from Chicago to Calgary, skied for two days at Lake Louise where there was little snow, and to compound the agony, there was a beer strike. Disappointed with conditions there, and wanting beer with dinner, drove to a restaurant near hot springs just on the other side of the provincial line, in British Columbia. Canadian provinces have much more autonomy than US states. In Alberta one only hears about things in Alberta.

In British Columbia all the literature is BC-oriented. On our table were the specifications for a brand new ski area called Panorama Mountain with an incredible vertical drop of 4000 feet! We decided on the spot to head in the direction of Invermere, the small town at the base of Panorama Mountain. It was my habit not to reserve motel rooms in advance so as to maximize flexibility during one-week trips we took to the west while Rose babysat the kids in Chicago. This strategy proved particularly helpful that year. We found ourselves the next morning at the base of Panorama Mountain. Ski lifts featured signs in English and Japanese. A new airport nearby was bringing skiers from Asia to this remote location.

It was necessary to take a rope tow from the base lodge, where lift tickets were sold, to the incredibly long chairlift that reached the top of the skiable terrain. The area was in the midst of construction. I could hear the hum of construction equipment. We were early arrivals at a great mountain in the process of being harnessed. The snow was much better than it had been in Lake Louise. It was bitterly cold on the long lift to the top. Near the top, I heard a different hum, the hum of helicopters. Taynton Bowl was home to a heli-ski operation, I learned that afternoon, in the bar when I got talking to a young man from New Zealand who was consoling his disappointment with drink. He had injured his wrist skiing that day and would be unable to join his heli-ski party for the rest of a week he had saved for, and anticipated for a year.

Dominique was not interested in skiing the next day because of the cold. He asked if I might be interested in taking his place. Absolutely. Who did I need to speak with? He pointed me in the right direction, and $100 secured me a spot. The next morning I was a newcomer among serious skiers, with topnotch equipment. I remember one woman who kept her face completely covered so as to remove any trace of being on a ski vacation, she explained to me when I asked.

The helicopter pilot had cut his teeth in Vietnam. He explained that flying in these mountains was far more dangerous. The wind could shift direction at a moments notice and send a copter crashing down a hillside. It was necessary to minimize time on the ground for that reason. We were instructed to deplane quickly as the copters bleeds kept turning, and our guides unloaded our skis from the basket in which they were carried, in military precision. There was also the danger of starting avalanches if any of us wandered beyond the boundaries our guides pointed out. The copter would fetch us at prearranged locations at the end of long runs and take us back to small landing zones at the top of majestic mountains. I documented this unforgettable day with color photos.

Several ski memories worth noting occurred soon after Amtrak moved me from Seattle to Chicago. On the Thanksgiving weekend of that year (1975) I took the train to Salt Lake City to visit my friend Elton. Elton did not ski, which I found hard to believe for an athletic young man who had grown up so close to the mountains that probably get the best powder on earth if not every year certainly on average, over time. They are high and able to squeeze the most moisture from the clouds that pass. The highest of the mountains, Alta, is easily accessible from Salt Lake, by car up the Cottonwood Canyon, a 45-minute drive. This makes for a perfect combination of cheap lodging, in the many motels in this large metropolis, and world-class mountains with fantastic snow if your timing is good.

I had met Elton in the Philippines. The two of us played on the faculty basketball team. I considered him an athlete. He told me he had never taken up skiing because he could not afford it when young. He was happy to provide me with lodging over the long weekend. I told Elton that I would be sleeping at his place but spending my days in the mountains. He said that would be OK.

When I got to Salt Lake it was raining hard in the valley. A blizzard was moving through the mountains. Talk about timing! I was excited. The local news was not good. The storm was so strong that the road up the canyon was closed, and was expected to remain closed for several days. The ski resorts were closed. I spent a frustrating Thanksgiving Day with Elton's family watching the Cowboys beat the Redskins on a last minute "hail Mary" pass by Clint Longley. This further depressed my spirits. I could not believe my bad luck, to be so close to those great mountains during the passing of a historic blizzard and having to watch for news for when the road up Cottonwood Canyon would be opened.

The next morning the reporter said that the storm was clearing, Snowbird was expected to open for people staying in the resort. Alta was hopelessly buried in snow and wouldn't be open for days. The authorities were doing everything possible to open the Canyon road but didn't expect to have it cleared until the evening. The only way into Snowbird that morning was by helicopter.

"Where would the helicopter take off from?", I asked Elton.

He wasn't sure but agreed to drive me in the most probable direction. Sure enough, we found the place and I paid I can't remember how much to get on, not believing my luck! I would hitch a ride down the mountain, I told Elton, or stay there if trapped. The copter deposited four passengers at Snowbird at about the time the lower mountain was opening. I had never seen such deep snow. The challenge was how to move through waist deep snow far enough to get to a place with sufficient slope that gravity would take over and you could begin a decent. The runs accessible by the lifts opened in the morning were hardly steep enough to make it worthwhile. There were not a lot of us struggling with these once in a lifetime conditions that morning.

Everyone was waiting to hear when the upper mountain would be opened up. This happened at around 11. I was in line with the locals lucky enough to be there. Many of them were equipped with snorkels in addition to goggles, to be able to breath, they explained. I will never again experience conditions that greeted me that day. No slope was too steep to ski. It was necessary to seek out, and drop into, the steepest sections of this rugged mountain to find terrain on which you could get enough velocity to make a run interesting!

During the next two hours I was in a dream, making fresh tracks on steeps that were visible from the chair on the ride back up. There was joyous shouting by those who did not have snorkels in their mouths. I experienced incredible somersaults, falling while going straight down, unafraid of speed. The depth of the snow kept velocity down, and falls were into clouds of snow. The main problem was the time it took to recover one's bearings and keep going.

Incredibly, I recognized a friend from DC in the lift line. He was staying at Snowbird. Would I join his group for lunch? I told him that I did not want to spend much time eating on a day like this but agreed to look for his party at the agreed to time at the mid-mountain restaurant. I got there a little late but found a seat.

I explained that I had just moved to Chicago. One of the members of the party said he was from Chicago.

"Glad to meet you. I work for Amtrak, what do you do there?"

"Work in television."

"OK. What's your name?"

"Walter Jacobson."

"Walter what?" The name meant nothing to me. I did not have a TV and didn't watch CBS news, learning only upon my return to Chicago that Walter Jacobson was part of the top rated news duo, along with Bill Curtis.

The road back to Salt Lake was open by the time that incredible day ended and I made it to Elton's that night where I had a good sleep, dreaming of what I had just experienced, pinching myself.

When transferred from Seattle to Chicago by Amtrak I was given the south side of Chicago as my territory. The locals preferred to visit the tonier north side, and western suburbs. This was OK with me. I learned that the major wholesaler of ski packages was located in my territory. Amtrak service provided access, from the east, to the mountains I had discovered from Seattle. In addition Chicago had overnight service to Denver on the San Francisco bound train, and access to Taos, in New Mexico, on the way to Los Angeles.

The wholesaler had sold a trip via rail to the AYH ski club to Taos. I decided to go along to get a first hand look at this destination. The group unloaded from the Southwest Chief after an overnight ride in the middle of a desert, in Lamy, New Mexico, where two buses were waiting for the trip to the mountains a couple of hours away. We drove through the historic village of Taos, full of art galleries, past the Indian pueblo on its outskirts, up into a ski bowl developed by Ernie Blake, the legendary pioneer of western American skiing, a Swiss mountain man who married Rhoda, a New York socialite, and brought her to the New Mexico wilderness, in 1955. Ernie flew around the mountains of the region and discovered perfect ski terrain underneath Kachina Peak, with a northern exposure that would hold snow late into the season. He and his bride moved into a camper and started to build a European style resort from scratch.

Ernie ran the place with Germanic discipline. Lifts closed for an hour at noon, to allow skiers to eat lunch in the lodges at the base where everyone had a package that included three meals. The AYH group was lodged in the St. Bernard, the lodge run by Jean Mayer, head of the ski school and master chef. Part of every Taos stay back then was a ski school package. Arrivals were grouped by skill on the first day and spent the mornings with their instructor and were free to ski on their own in the afternoon.

These rules were explained to me on the bus ride up by veterans of previous Taos stays. As we approached the mountain I could not believe my luck. It was snowing. It snowed all night. We awoke to a fairy tale like scene. A foot and a half of fresh powder covered the mountain. One reason Taos has a reputation as an expert mountain is that Al's run, one of the steepest runs on the mountain, climbs up from the base lodges, and is visible to everyone riding chair #1 that leads to the upper mountain where many of the intermediate runs are located.

There was plenty of fresh powder to ski that morning at the top of the mountain. As the top became skied out, I decided to check out Al's run, the slope I remembered seeing on my ride up. There were ropes closing off access at the top of the chair, for no good reason, I thought. There was certainly no avalanche risk, given the terrain that I had seen. The ski patrol was shooting cannon into snow pack in Kachina Bowl to release any dangerous accumulations there, but the run under the lift (I didn't know its name at the time) seemed like a part of the mountain that was ready for exploration.

I did not cross under any ropes, but dropped into the run from below, after skiing through some trees. What a magnificent time I had on my first run down! I fell a couple of times, creating not only the first tracks but several big face plant holes. As I was gathering myself after these falls people on the lift were shouting things to me that I did not understand. I picked up the notion that I might be in some sort of trouble. Nothing to do but continue down one of the most special runs in North America!

As I approached the bottom of the lift I noticed a man in a yellow outfit, including a flat hat of European styling, standing at the base of the hill. I was out of breath, huffing and puffing, thinking back on one of the most memorable descents of my life. The man walked towards me and grabbed the lift ticket that was hanging around my neck. I knew I was in trouble.

"You must be Ernie Blake," I said. "I was looking forward to meeting you under different circumstances. My name is Martti Vallila, a Finnish name. I am an Amtrak rep here with the AYH ski club. Sorry if I have made some mistake, but the top of the mountain has been pretty well skied out, and I could not leave this wonderful section untouched."

Ernie let go of my lift ticket and began to smile. "You know you crossed some lines. This run is closed!"

"Why? There is no avalanche danger."

"We were planning to film on this run in a while. So you are here with Amtrak. I like the trains. Most of the mountains I skied in Switzerland were accessible by train."

Ernie the businessman saw that I not only had chutzpah but could be a valuable contact. I explained that I was staying at the St. Bernard. He showed me his apartment, a few meters away, and invited me for a drink at the end of the ski day. So began a friendship that culminated in his gift to me on the day of my wedding. Dominique and I were his guests at the ski area for our second honeymoon, the one following my first week at IBM. I paid for lodging, but the lift tickets were on him.

Ernie loosened his hold on the mountain over time. He kept the lifts running over lunch hour, first on weekends, and then every day. Taos was one of the last resorts to allow snow boarding, long after the rest of the world had converted. It remains, in my opinion, the best destination resort in North America. When you enter Taos Ski Village you exit the rest of the world. Packages including the mandatory ski school are still in force, as far as I know, contributing to the ski school's reputation as #1 in America.

Ernie did not insist that Dominique and I participate in ski school the week of our honeymoon, allowing me time to introduce Dominique to the mountain alone. I skied forbidden portions of Taos with Steve McKinney, who Ernie considered a "wild man". My last visit (to date) was during my cross-country drive from North Carolina to San Francisco in my red Toyota. I was driving to San Francisco to take repossession of my dream house from the tenants who had occupied it for six years while my daughters completed their schooling in North Carolina and I built my Russian business (as described in "Bannana in Russia").

I drove in for the day, which happened to be Ernie's birthday. He had died several years earlier, but there was a firework display that night, in his honor. I ate a great meal served by my friend Jean Meyer, before continuing my drive into the wilderness in the direction of Colorado. I had taken this cross-country route especially to pop in on Taos. My plan was to rejoin 80 by crossing some of the most desolate area accessible by road in North America. I remember the flashing red oil light on the dashboard lighting up as I drove into Taos to fill my car with gas for my journey into the night. I would drive as far as I could before finding a place to sleep.

Why I did not add oil to the engine, I do not know. Perhaps my thinking was affected by fatigue from the full day of skiing, or from the wine I had with Jean's wonderful meal. I left the station with a full tank wondering where I would spend the night. A half hour out of town the Toyota came to a screeching halt. The engine had locked up! It was dark. I was in the middle of nowhere. Not a single car in either direction. The wind was howling. Imagining wild animals in the surrounding forest was easy. I pulled my sleeping bag from the trunk and tried to find comfort in the car, filled with things and skis.

After a while, finding it impossible to fall asleep in such cramped quarters, I was ready to risk the outdoors. I opened the sleeping bag along the length of the car (that I had managed to move off the paved road). Don't know how much I slept that night. Morning took forever to arrive. Drifting in and out of sleep I was kicking myself for ignoring the warning my car had given me, what would I now do, if I were not devoured by wolves, or some other wild creatures. In the middle of the night nature called, and I was forced to exit the comfort of my sleeping bag to relieve myself. I can think of no shit I have taken in more difficult circumstances, shivering, shaking from the cold, after finding a proper place, then taking a long time to reheat my surroundings, after cleaning myself with the help of surrounding snow.

I was grateful to be alive at sunrise. No sign of any traffic on this desolate road. Finally I spotted a car coming from the direction I had been traveling. I stepped into the road, forcing the driver to stop. The nervous man could see my desperate condition and agreed to give me a ride into town where he left me off at a station with a tow truck. I explained to the attendant roughly where I thought the car was and we negotiated the cost of a tow into town. I was beyond the limit of any AAA coverage and would have to pay in cash. The final charge would depend on the mileage, he explained. His garage also handled the U Haul concession in town, I learned as we chatted on the drive to my car. From my description of events he was pretty sure my engine had locked up. It would probably have to be replaced. Used Toyota engines were shipped to California. Ordering one, and getting it to Taos could probably be done in two weeks.

Two weeks!

My rush to California was fatally delayed by my stupidity. If only I had put oil in that engine. It was speaking to me. How could I have ignored the warning? What kind of an omen was this for the start of my new California adventure? What would I possibly do to occupy myself in Taos for the (at least) two weeks it would take to get an engine? These were some of my thoughts as we drove my crippled car into town. The mechanic said he would need some time to validate his hypothesis. He would need to make some calls to California to check delivery times for relevant engines. He told me to acquaint myself with the town I would probably be spending some time in, pointing out streets I should check out if I was interested in finding a low cost motel.

I followed his advice. I took the bus into the center of town and was struck by the strong Indian content of the population. Got into a conversation with an American Indian on the bus, an expert firefighter, used to being summoned to locations throughout the west on short notice. American Indians form a large portion of the front line of America's firefighting force, my new friend explained. Just as their secret language was a front line during the Second World War, I responded, gaining his respect. He pointed out a motel I should check out. I got off the bus and made an inquiry. They had a room available. Weekly rates were reasonable.

I was armed with this knowledge when I returned to the garage where the news was not good. My engine was, in fact, locked, requiring replacement. Calls to contacts in California had not yet identified any engine that could be shipped, but new information was expected soon. My car, a Corolla, was among Toyota's most popular models, and there were lots of appropriate engines arriving in the US, made available by the Japanese habit of changing engines just before their warranties expired.

I noticed the garage had a U Haul truck on the lot.

"Will that truck pull a car trolley?" I asked. It could, but unfortunately the garage had no car trolleys available, was the mechanics answer. He checked his computer.

"There may be a trolley coming in later today."

Rather then wait for an engine from California, why not haul my car to California, my destination, I hypothesized.

Where in California was I going?

San Francisco.

The mechanic looked through a book and identified a garage in San Francisco specializing in Toyotas. He called them, was told they could have an engine available by the time I got there. In that moment my plan was transformed. Now it was a matter of when the car tow would arrive so it could be attached to the shortest U Haul able to tow a car. Luck turned in my direction. The car trolley arrived before sundown and was attached to a 16-foot truck that I filled (barely) with the contents of my Toyota. I could sleep in the cab or inside the truck.

My arrival in San Francisco was not the triumphant return that I had envisioned when I left Raleigh in my convertible. I arrived, three days after leaving Taos (I took the scenic route, up highway 1 from Los Angeles) dragging my car to a garage where it took a week to get rejuvenated. My only consolation was knowing how much worse things could have been, in that Taos motel, waiting for an engine from California to arrive.

***

The most *memorable* skiing day of my life?

The deep powder day at Snowbird, previously described, is rivaled by a day I had at Jackson Hole some years later. I was there with the family. We had a place for the week, eating many of our meals at the Mangy Moose. It was my first visit to a place I had long imagined, the mountain with the longest vertical drop in the US. I discovered this spectacular mountain during a week with Dominique and the kids. It was their spring break and conditions were good. We spotted a live moose from a chair during a ride.

Skiing vacations with my kids are among the happiest times of my life. Both girls learned to ski in Val d'Isere, France, during my days there with IBM. The commite d'enterprise packages made family skiing affordable and the

French know how to teach this stuff! It was not long before the kids were following me into the "magic forest", Sofia skiing in Kristine's tracks. The week in Jackson Hole had been magical.

The family flew back to Chicago a day before I did, giving me a day alone at Jackson Hole. By that time I knew the mountain. I was back in shape and in rhythm. I skied the gondola, from the base to the top, all day, descending fast enough to catch the same gondola I had ridden up! How many vertical feet I skied that day I cannot imagine. Certainly the most vertical feet I have skied on any day in my life. These days an iPhone app provides the answer to such questions. I do not recall falling once on that magical day on the mountain.

As I walked through the parking lot, exhausted, at the end of that day, I slipped on a sheet of ice I did not see, falling with skis in hand, and landing awkwardly, thankfully not hitting my head. My closest brush that day with a "near death experience" was in the parking lot at the end of an incredible day, at an unexpected moment in an unexpected place.

My snow skiing escapades were cut short suddenly one spring day on Squaw Valley's Red Dog lift. I was skiing in the trees alone, in heavy wet snow, and forced my right leg to turn. I knew immediately that I had injured my knee. I did not know how seriously. I was able to make it to the bottom and limp to the car, drive to San Francisco where I was in the middle of renovating my dream house. I had just left IBM so I had no medical coverage. I left it to nature, thinking my knee would heal itself. I was sufficiently mobile to continue the demolition and sheet rocking my house demanded. The urgency of that project took my attention off my knee. I adjusted my walk to compensate for the pain that soon dissolved into discomfort.

That injury prevented me from skiing for the next six years and probably saved my life. I stopped at a time I was taking many risks on the mountain, skiing the trees where I could find my beloved powder snow, without a helmet. I had the knee looked at when I returned to San Francisco, after selling our North Carolina home, and enrolling in the Kaiser health plan. My ACL was torn. I had an operation that repaired it. The years I had been protecting my weak knee had an effect on my hip. I had a hip replacement as a result, at a fairly young age. Finally repaired I regained strength in my right leg and returned to skiing, wearing a brace on my right knee.

I no longer need the brace and now ski wearing a helmet, like almost everyone on the mountain these days. I do get into the trees occasionally, but no longer risk my life the way I once did, content to speed down groomed slopes most of the time, in my wise old age. My main pleasure in this life-long sport has become teaching the next generation.

***

I conclude the skiing section of this book by taking the reader back to my water skiing days. There were not any near death experiences in the three summers I operated my water skiing business with my Zodiac. I suppose the fact that I was able to operate, and grow, the business can be interpreted as successfully dodging the fate of most start-ups: death.

The key to my success was repeat business, not only from the McKinney's but from many people, some of who became life long friends. Seth Tillman, an aid to Senator Fulbright, came to me as a two-ski man. I taught him to slalom. We talked politics while he rested between rides. He became a family friend. Rose sold him a house in Foxhall Village. Seth took me to lunch one day in the Senate dining room where I had some of the famous bean soup. I just missed crossing paths with another young aid of Fulbright's, a Bill Clinton. (Seth wrote one of Clinton's recommendations for law school.)

We became guests at the Rehoboth Beach house Seth rented with other DC staff members. It was at Seth's house that I met Dominique, my wife, in 1976. I was visiting DC over the Labor Day weekend from Chicago and Rose and I were Seth's guests at a different beach house from the one we had stayed in years before. Dominique was invited for Labor Day weekend by another of Seth's friends and I admit to stealing her during that weekend, after she saw me attempt to navigate the first slalom course I had ever encountered, talked her into flying to Chicago where we were married three months later.

Seth was not the only politically connected parson I met through my business. On the morning of August 22, 1968 I had a woman and young son as customers. We got to talking, as was my habit with new acquaintances. (I found some skiers uninterested in discussion, thinking of me as an appendage of my strange boat. Others treated me as a human being, which was the case that morning.) I mentioned that I was born in Prague. The woman asked if I knew what had just happened in Czechoslovakia. I told her that I did not. Czechoslovakia has just been invaded by Russian troops. Her husband, Helmut Sonnenfeldt, was not with her because he was in DC dealing with the situation. I did not know who Mr. Sonnenfeldt was that day, learning only later that he was considered "Kissinger's Kissinger".

A well-known British journalist I shall call Henry arrived one day with his girlfriend. What made their visit memorable was the moment, during our return to the marina after Henry had skied while his girlfriend observed, when she stood up and her bikini pants remained stuck to the rubber of the Zodiac's inflatable tubes, which doubled as seats. She did not notice until Henry, in a demonstration of British understatement, said "Dear, you need to pull your pants up."

I sometimes encountered persons who had difficulty deciding, among them, who would ski first. I learned to solve this problem by saying that I would volunteer to hold a number of fingers in my fist. The person who guessed the number would have to jump into the water. One day I took two girls out on the boat who claimed to be witches. At least one of them, as I recall. Neither wanted to ski first. I explained my method for resolving such questions. The witch said it was easy to read my mind and guessed the right number. She thought that this meant she would ski second. I explained that the person who guessed correctly skied first. She was not pleased.

That evening as I was taking the Zodiac to the berth she occupied at night I got too close to a piling at low tide and the boat scraped against an exposed barnacle that caused a scratch that deflated the tube I was sitting on. I had a hunch the angry witch had something to do with it. It took me a couple of days to patch the Zodiac (who survived a "near death experience") and resume my operation. Some months later I ran into the witch in Georgetown and told her about the incident. She smiled, knowingly.

Money from my water skiing business combined with scholarships, $1000 from the DC school system and aid from Stanford allowed me to graduate without any debt. Tuition at Stanford was less than $2000 a year. I lived off campus after the second quarter of my sophomore year in frugal arrangements with housemates. My senior year cost only one quarter's tuition, as I completed my social thought honors thesis while skiing on snow.

Not being in debt gave me the freedom to do anything I wanted when I graduated. I ended up with a teaching job in the Philippines that paid $60 a month. More on that soon enough.

Community organizing in Alabama

The summer after my sophomore year I wanted to do something socially responsible and instructive. I learned about the Southern Rural Research Project, a summer program providing community-organizing opportunities in Alabama for whites interested in seeing the south from a black perspective. Orientation was conducted in Selma, the place that gained the civil rights movement a place in the consciousness of the nation. Martin Luther King's march across the bridge was met with water cannon and dogs and cameras. I drove there in a recently acquired Volkswagen beetle with two Stanford friends going east. I remember the three of us stopping for lunch in Flagstaff, Arizona at a cafeteria where we chose our food from options displayed behind glass. As we were moving through the line, a man asked:

"Are you guys from the circus?"

My first reaction was to wonder if there was anything about the way we looked to suggest such a query. I realized that the question was probably innocently posed in friendship to three new faces, given the fact that a circus *had* just moved into town.

Participants were welcomed in Selma (on the wrong side of the tracks) by Uz Nunelley and his white girlfriend. Uz was a master driver on dirt roads, I would learn. After a week-long orientation program in Selma during which we learned about the federal housing programs that we were expected to explain to eligible black families, we were taken to the families who would house us. Uz had me follow him in my VW, out of town on a paved road, and, about half way to Prattville, we turned off, in the middle of Autauga County, onto red dirt roads that eventually led to the home of Hezikaih and Etta Tytus. The one story wooden building with a tin root and front porch looked hand built.

Hezikaih came out on the porch to greet us. Uz introduced me to him as "Martus". Hezikaih wore overalls made of blue denim and a cotton shirt with a red and white pattern. His large stomach filled the overalls. His face shined with both a broad smile and a skin tone that reflected the sun. We went inside to meet Etta. She was shy, a bit shorter than her husband, wore a light blue and white dress. They showed me the bedroom where I would be sleeping. I felt comfortable. Uz left, telling me he would be back later to check on how things were going.

Hezikaih took me out back and showed me the pen where his pigs lived. He went in and fed them, putting meal in a trough and adding water. He told me he followed the Atlanta Braves, thought that Hank Aaron was the greatest player of all. Etta told me she liked to cook peach cobbler pie. Hezikaih told me she was a great cook, which I soon discovered, when we sat down to our first meal of fried chicken and beans, followed by peach cobbler dessert.

Why was I there? They "aksed".

To see conditions in the south for myself, I explained. I had grown up in DC, was hearing about activities in the south aimed at improving the lives of poor people there and wanted to do something useful. Maybe you can fix the leak in our roof, volunteered Hezikaih. I would see what I could do the next day, I promised.

Next morning I climbed to the roof with some tar and placed it on spots I thought might be responsible for a leak. While I was on the roof a tractor driven by a white man drove by. The man stared at me. When I came down Hezikaih laughed, said he had never seen such a look of disbelief on the face of Mr. Henderson, a local big shot landowner. "He just about drove his tractor off the road, staring at a white boy on my roof!"

I got acquainted with members of the community through baseball.

"You play?" I was asked by Junior, a kid about my age.
"Yes, a little bit."
"What position?"
"Well, my favorite position is catcher."

"I'll be! That's my position too. Why don't you join us on Sunday when we play after church."

"Sure enough."

I started Sunday at the church service, sitting next to the Tytus' who wore their Sunday bests. We listened to the preacher almost sing his sermon. Most of the all black congregation kept cool waving cardboard fans with pictures of JFK, RFK or MLK on them. I was to experience church services in various churches that summer, and listen to a number of preachers, who, after arriving in fancy cars, roused their congregations into a spiritual frenzy I have never experienced anywhere else. At more than one service I saw worshipers "entered by the spirit" and fall to the ground. The singing interaction between the preacher and the congregation starts slowly, and proceeds to an emotional release that you have to experience to understand.

After church the community gathered around a field not far from the church. The infield was etched into the sparse grass by use. The bases were flat grey sacks folded into a square. Most spectators stood outside the lines of play. There were a few wooden benches, and some people brought folding chairs.

"Let's put whitey behind the plate," suggested Junior. I was invited to warm up our pitcher. This kid could throw! One for a fastball, two for a curve, three for a change-up. We agreed on our signals. The game against a team from a nearby town started in late afternoon, once the heat had dissipated. It was interrupted often by the need to retrieve a foul ball from the surrounding woods.

I am not much of a ball player. Enjoy catching because its the most active position and involves trying to outsmart the batter. I have never caught a better pitcher than the fire-baller who followed my instructions that day. His curve dropped like you see on TV. I called a lot of curves and change ups, because it hurt to catch his fastball. Hitting is not my strong suite. I did manage a single, between first and second, that first game. In my second, I got lucky and a hard swing connected perfectly with a ball thrown at great velocity, producing the longest hit of my life, which wasn't a hit because it was caught by the center fielder as he ran as far back as he could. I couldn't believe how far I had hit the ball, but kept my astonishment to myself, hoping that I would be able to repeat the feat. That freak drive moved me up in the batting order for a few games, to fifth, before it was understood that my shot had been a fluke.

After ball games there was partying. The music I remember was from The Jackson Five. When I asked about the origin of what we were drinking, I was told it was moonshine, cooked in a bathtub. Delivering moonshine is at the heart of the NASCAR racing tradition in the south. Locals became expert at evading the police on dirt roads. One day when I was driving with Uz he explained that he was master of a key maneuver, the 180-degree turn. Driving at high speed on a dirt road kicks up a lot of dust. If the driver is able to execute a 180-degree turn, by swirling the car in just the right way, he suddenly turns against his pursuer who sees a car coming at him from the dust. The dust then suddenly disappears. The car being chased has vanished!

Uz then illustrated the maneuver. I had to admit it required daring and skill. Uz could hotwire just about any car in a few seconds, he assured me. Most men in Autauga County knew about cars. This came in handy because not long after arrival my car had engine trouble. Lots of people chipped in with opinions on who was in the best position to help. Can't remember now the details of how my VW was fixed, just that it was up on the blocks in back yards for a considerable amount of time.

Life in the Tytus home was peaceful. I would wake up at sunrise with the cry of roosters. There were chickens in addition to pigs in the back yard that needed feeding in the morning and evening. We ate fresh vegetables from the small garden, expertly prepared, and drank tea. People stayed inside during the heat of the day. One day I volunteered to go okra picking along with many of the youngsters. A southern delicacy often found in gumbo, okra came to the US on slave ships from West Africa. It must be picked by hand. We were fetched at sunrise by a truck and taken to a field, given baskets, and pointed in the direction of rows in need of harvesting.

Most pickers wore gloves to protect them from the tiny scales of the okra plant that must be snapped, individually, from the stem. It took me twice as long to fill a basket than some of the eight-year olds I was competing with. They saw the plants better, were closer to the height of the plants, and had practiced dexterity in their little fingers. We gathered at the end of the day in a line to be paid according to the number of buckets we had brought to the white farmer, the production of each picker was recorded both my himself, and checked against statistics written down. There were no discrepancies between the two counts, as far as I could tell. I was embarrassed at the low number I had to say out loud and don't remember how much payment I received. Every time I eat okra, a delicacy, I think back to that day.

One of the most dynamic people I was introduced to was Sally Hadnot (her real name), a local civil rights leader. She wanted her young son to integrate local swimming pools but first Sonny had to learn how to swim. She trusted me, who she called Tarzan, with this job. I took Sonny to a pool, explained that he needed to jump in and start moving his arms and legs in circular motions, treading water. He immediately ran to the diving board, jumped off, sank like a rock to the bottom, where I went to retrieve him.

"Why didn't you move your arms and legs like I told you?" I asked.

"I got nervous and forgot that part!" was his answer.

We got along fine after that and Sonny was swimming before I left. He took me to places he said might have water moccasins and dared me to go in, along with him. I did.

Was that a "near death experience"? I had others that certainly qualify.

Sally invited me to accompany her, a white woman colleague of hers, and a black man who owned a fast Chevrolet to a ceremony in a small town west of Selma to celebrate the first election of a black official. It took us a couple of hours to get there. The ceremony involved speeches by local officials, including Julian Bond, and a meal, beneath tents, for more than a hundred people. We started home shortly before sunset. Just west of Selma we decided to stop to get something to drink at a small grocery store at the corner of two crossing two lane roads, that must have been a local gathering spot judging from the cars parked around it. Our driver maneuvered his Camaro into a spot not far from the screened entrance of the store and I volunteered to go in to purchase some soda. A bell rang as I opened the screen door.

I bought a couple of cokes from the white man behind the counter and when I returned to our car noticed that another car had maneuvered behind ours. The occupants of that car claimed that they were stuck and could not move. I walked back into the store, explained our situation to the owner who came out and said something about letting us go on. The engine in the car behind started. So did the engines of several other cars. We were allowed to leave but were then followed, in the direction of Selma, on a dark road, without lights.

Our driver increased his speed. The car behind us tried to pass us on the left. We maneuvered into the center of the road to prevent this. Sally was with me in the back seat.

"You see, Martus, this is what we face!" she was shouting. Our interracial car had attracted the attention of persons who wanted to do us harm.

"What in the world are these people thinking? What do they want to do?" I was saying out loud, in disbelief, as we bounced at high speed into the night, maneuvering from side to side to prevent the first car of a caravan of at least four from getting to either side of us.

"I wish I had my piece with me!" shouted Sally.

A car approached from the opposite direction. Sally took out a white handkerchief rolled down her window and waved it to the passing car. A local signaling system, she explained. Our pursuers lost interest as we approached the lights of Selma. We were able to slow down. I couldn't process what had just happened, don't know how close to a "near death experience" I had survived. It still seems more like something out of a movie than something I saw up close.

Hezikaih and I watched the all-star game together. I couldn't help but reflect on the fact that the baseball I played that summer was probably closer to the origins of the game then what we saw broadcast from the Houston Astrodome, played on an artificial surface. I gave the Tytus' my address in DC at the end of the summer. Rose received a letter from Etta about a year later explaining that Hezikaih had passed away.

What did I learn that summer?

There was great skepticism in the black community about the government housing programs. Worry that by signing up, they risked losing homes they had. Many of the older citizens had seen their children go north, to find conditions more difficult than what they knew in the south.

Don't know if I accomplished anything beyond my goal of gaining a personal perspective on life in the south from a black point of view. We experienced several violent thunderstorms that summer that rattled the tin roof, but no water entered the Tytus home after my visit to their roof.

My car was fixed in time so that I could drive to Atlanta for the NAACP convention (as an official delegate) with three colleagues. We drove there in a mixed-race car, but did not experience the harassment of that night outside Selma. It was a visit full of contrasts. I slept in a home with a black child that cried all night, for lack of food I was told. Another night we had drinks at the top of one of the hotels with a circulating bar. I listened to the seemingly endless keynote speech delivered by George McGovern, who was running for president, that was followed by impromptu remarks by Muhammad Ali, in town preparing for a title fight and called up from the audience. Ali's remarks mesmerized a crowd that McGovern had almost put to sleep.

Another mesmerizing speaker that summer was a young Jesse Jackson. My next visit to Atlanta was in 1977, for IBM training. Driving into town then, from Chicago, I thought back to the parts of town I had been privileged to experience during that summer in Alabama, as a community organizer. I was living then in the city where a future president of the United States did his community organizing, about which there will be more mention later...

Stanford and exploring California

The only near death experience I associate with my campus days at Stanford (I hit the tree at Mt. Rose while a student there) was the night I left my dorm at Grove House by bicycle to mail a letter. A car stopped at the sign as I approached the intersection of Campus Drive I needed to cross to get to the post office. Unseen by me the car behind passed the stopped car on its right, and appeared to me just as it hit me.

Fortunately the pedal on the car side of the bike was in the up position, allowing me to slide off the bike by instinctively placing my hand onto the car's hood, instead of being dragged under the car along with my bike. My head cracked the windshield. The car jarred to a stop pushing me onto the street. The spider web windshield pattern was probably more frightening to the driver, who thought he had killed someone, than it was to me when I saw it, knowing I had survived. I rubbed my head and didn't feel anything wrong. I was pissed about losing my bike. The driver got out, nervously asked if I was OK.

"I think so. But you have totaled my bike!"

"I have a bike I will give you as a replacement."

I got the drivers name walked to the post office where I mailed my letter returned to Grove house and went to sleep. The next evening, in line for dinner, I was telling some friends about the accident I had the night before.

"Your head cracked the windshield? Really? You need to go to the hospital and have your head examined" was the unanimous advice of my friends, some of whom were pre-meds and aware of the time it sometimes takes for signs of head trauma to appear. Several agreed to drive me to Stanford Hospital where I was subjected to appropriate examination. A policeman arrived and asked me to fill out an accident report. The driver was contacted and asked to appear. Results from the tests were negative. I was, indeed, OK.

The driver asked the policeman what to do about the windshield. Why don't you park the car somewhere in East Palo Alto and go to a movie, and announce an accident while you were away was the advice given him. The bike I got in exchange was slightly sturdier than the one I had lost, so I was happy.

One of the places I lived off campus was in a house in East Palo Alto. I shared the rent with four housemates but was somewhat separate from them. The house included a water tower, the interior of which became my residence. Accessible only by ladder my perch provided peace and quiet, as well as a good view, from the top floor, the only place to live. Security was lousy but I didn't have much of value to the kids who would occasionally climb up to visit.

All of my off-campus residences were somewhat unusual. My first was a converted garage of a small home occupied by Michael and his girlfriend Eleanor, who was girlfriend of a girlfriend of mine, Sabra. Michael was a leader of the revolutionary forces that had momentum on campus at the height of the Vietnam War. He had been a university insider, student representative on many committees, but got so disenchanted with the establishment that he refused to graduate. He became a Marxist-Leninist activist.

Student body president the year before I got to Stanford was David Harris, credited with starting the resistance to the draft movement on the West Coast. He married Joan Baez. I ran into Harris once, in Marc Mancall's Grove House seminar during my freshman year. The seminar was on "revolution". Mancall was trying to replicate the Harvard house system at Stanford and instituted a system in which all residents of Grove House took seminars taught by Grove House "fellows", Mancall being the biggest "fellow" (he weighed over 250 pounds). I was the only freshman to sign up for this intimidating man's revolution seminar. Many Grove residents were scared of this huge man who spoke seven or eight languages. French, Chinese, Russian,

Finnish, Italian, English are the ones I am sure of. There were others.

I didn't say a word for five weeks, listening instead to the philosophizing of the upperclassmen enrolled (Grove included a mix of all classes and sexes) and occasional special guest, like Harris. Mancall invited futurist Buckminster Fuller to Grove House before a speech he was scheduled to make. I remember his eyeballs completely filling the glasses he wore as he spoke to the group that joined him for lunch. I had never heard of him before that day. I found his brief talk so fascinating that I insisted on sitting in the front row of Memorial Auditorium for his lecture.

I learned that afternoon that Fuller's method at lectures was to pick out some members of the audience and begin to address them, instead of looking generally into the audience, as most public speakers do. The auditorium had a large crowd when Fuller started his lecture on his version of human history, the distribution of resources on the globe, the principles behind his geodesic dome design, a lecture he was delivering to me and the guy sitting next to me. My neighbor was so enthralled that he asked a question, which Fuller responded to.

Much of what Fuller was saying was incoherent due to poor amplification of his soft voice and the abstractness of his subject. Many students apparently began leaving the auditorium. I was mesmerized, didn't notice any exodus until the lecture ended and I saw a near empty auditorium. Buckminster Fuller was certainly one of a kind.

When I moved off campus I tried to replicate a small version of the Grove tradition in my third residence, on Cowper street, that I shared with two women and two man (my room was a converted exterior porch). We rotated cooking duties, one of us in charge for each day of the week. On my day I occasionally invited a professor to join us. A memorable dinner was with Walter Sokel, a German expert in existentialism whose course I took spring quarter of freshman year. He introduced me to Kierkegaard, Rilke, Kafka, Sartre, and Camus. I saw him two years later, eating lunch alone at Tressider Union, and invited him to join us. I had never taken a course from biologist Joshua Lederberg (later president of the Rockefeller Institute), but heard a lecture of his and was inspired to invite him. Both of these big thinkers appreciated the chance to sit around an off-campus dinner table.

Another memorable event during those Cowper street days was the Saturday I travelled to Altamont to witness what started out as Woodstock West but was transformed into an event remembered for the death of a spectator by the Hells Angels who were providing security for the event. Getting there from Palo Alto took a couple of hours. I parked my car miles from the site of the concert, realizing that finding parking closer was unlikely, and relied on hitching a ride, also unlikely, given the number of people walking in my direction, and the fullness of passing cars. But my karma was good (as was said in those days) and a passing car stopped, made space for me.

Getting close to the stage was out of the question because of the thick crowd already gathered around the stage in a valley. I settled on a hill with a direct view of the stage, making it possible to see and hear the performers, if only as distant stick figures. Behind the stage were huge speakers projecting the music to the surrounding hills containing more than 300,000. Much of the Altamont "experience" (as with Woodstock) was local, observing and meeting the collection of gathered free spirits, partaking in the weed that was circulating, listening to wandering bards. I remember a costumed "General Waste-More-Land", plastic airplanes protruding from his head, moving among the crowd.

A series of performers appeared on the distant stage. The Jefferson Airplane, Crosby, Stills, Nash & Young provided background music for the show going on all around. The Grateful Dead were on the program but suddenly cancelled. We were all waiting for the main event, the arrival of the Rolling Stones. The sun was allowed to set, creating additional drama. The helicopter rumored to be carrying the Stones could be heard, then seen, landing not far from the stage. There appeared to be a flurry of activity around the stage. Rumors about some problems began spreading through the crowd. I could see Hells Angels around the stage, couldn't make out what was going on.

"There has been a killing! By the Angels," was circulating. The Stones took the mike and asked for calm, then started playing music, "Sympathy for the Devil", "Jumping Jack Flash"....the crowd around me was moving, dancing, the scent of marijuana all around.

I learned what had happened in front of my eyes only after returning to Palo Alto the next day. My karma got me back to my car. I got a ride and got off close to where I had parked. Four people died at Altamont, one knifed by Hells Angels as he charged the stage with a gun, two from traffic accidents, a fourth in a drowning. There had been confrontations between the Angels surrounding the stage and some of the performers before the Stones arrived. Mick Jagger was punched soon after he exited the helicopter. The Hells Angels had been promised $500 of beer for security they were asked to provide (by surrounding the stage). They drank their beer during the day. The mayhem of the concert poisoned the hippie "peace and love" energy of Woodstock, four months earlier, and cast a harder edge to the hippy movement reflecting conditions in San Francisco's Height Ashbury District that became its epicenter.

Does that day qualify as a near death experience? In the sense that I was not far from the deaths of others, and had witnessed an event that would be seen as the moment the "peace and love" hippie movement died, yes.

***

My Stanford days ended with the delivery my honors thesis, written in the mountains while skiing, to Mancall. It was entitled "Negativism". The essential idea was that the scientific method was founded on the negative: "p is what not p is not" is how Mancall used to explain it. Another way of thinking about it is that the goal of the scientific method is to isolate *the* cause, through systematic *exclusion* of alternatives. No question about the *material* progress this method has produced. I was wondering about the effect of this thinking on the psyche, on social relations, on the "softer side" of life.

Can't say I had any answers, just questions, to which I was seeking some perspective. This led me to a curiosity about Asia, which I suspected had a different gestalt, and my decision to go to the Philippines, which will be discussed in detail later in this book.

***

My days at Stanford were the first of several stays in California during subsequent periods of my life. Aside from skiing incidents in its mountains, I experienced few near death experiences there of the physical sort.

I experienced a near death of the financial sort years later at the hands of one of Silicon Valley's high profile billionaires, Vinod Khosla, that inspired "Bannana in the Legal Gulag". I met Vladimir Poponin, a brilliant, exotic Russian inventor (who was obsessed with the grand challenge of rapidly reading the human genome) at the housewarming for my dream house on the top of Vallejo Street. We decided to become partners in commercializing his technology. Khosla got interested in Poponin's technology but rather than deal with me he launched a legal assault employing top-drawer legal talent (from Fenwick & West) to try to crush me.

The deceptions practiced by Khosla's legal team are illustrated in my book. I discovered, years after tangling with Khosla in court (and winning) that he had a subsequent dispute with Poponin in which his submission to the court concerning agreements he had with Poponin made false statements by his lawyers in the case against me that he was funding on Poponin's behalf.

Rather then recognize my legitimate rights, this supposed champion (according to the website of Khosla Ventures) of "those who dare to think outside the box" tried to destroy me with legal maneuver *insisting* all the while *on remaining anonymous*. The shameful story is told in "Bannana in the Legal Gulag". In retrospect (of the dot-connecting-kind) I see that my legal tangles with Khosla were preparation for near death struggles of the legal sort that awaited, in Finland.

The story of my struggle to keep my dream house on Vallejo Street is a near death experience of the financial variety that I describe in "Bannana in Boston". Here I add a few details of how I thought I had lost the house three times, before finally doing so. I saw the house for the first time shortly after seeing Russia for the first time. Both of these were life-changing moments I could not pass up.

My visit to Leningrad was possible, from Helsinki, in 1991, because a Russian boat was in the harbor, one cabin was still vacant and its four berths available to accommodate my wife and two daughters without visas because we would be sleeping not in Leningrad but rather on the Kuznetsov, in the harbor, while touring the city for two days.

That look at Russia, on the summer it was being born, or reborn, introduced me to the purpose that would guide the rest of my life. The light Steve Jobs would describe years later in his Stanford address went off in my head. I saw energy, an enthusiasm, and a potential in that country from the application of an outside perspective that I was in a position to contribute to, because of things I had experienced in my life up to then.

Born on the inside of the Iron Curtain, in Prague, and having been educated on the outside, aware that Finland had historically played a role as intermediary between these worlds, convinced that communication technologies were creating the possibility, in fact, the inevitability of a permanent connection between the giant countries of

Russia and America, I recognized a geopolitical opportunity and responsibility.

If not now, when? If not me, who? *How* was the big question to which I did not have an answer, other than to tap into my Finnish roots. I visited San Francisco a few months later on a business trip from North Carolina near what I sensed would be the end of my period of "preparation" at IBM. I had started with International Business Machines with a focus on the first letter, in Chicago, in new account sales, in a new division, selling small computers to anyone I could convince in a territory that included portions of downtown Chicago, at a time Chicago was emerging on the world stage as an international city. My five years of selling for the General Systems Division (during which I earned five 100% clubs and one "golden circle") prepared me for promotion to a staff job that I insisted be in the international side of the business.

Big blue accommodated my wishes by sending me to New York for a two-year assignment in "national language support". It became my job to coordinate implementations of the entire (accented) character sets of languages at the moment computers were being asked to fully support them (with the emergence of text applications), across three different IBM platforms that had developed independently, the data processing division (DPD), the word processing division (WP) and the newest general systems division (GSD). Becoming an internal expert in this conversion, in a part of the company that included Hebrew and Arabic (but not Kanji or Chinese) got me a ticket to Paris when the new Area's Division was formed and headquartered in the IBM tower in La Defense. What began as a two-year assignment from Chicago to New York became a five-year departure from Chicago, the last three of which we spent in Paris.

It was a perfect time for a move to France for the family. The kids discovered that French was not only a language spoken by their mother, and imitated (poorly) by their father, but a language spoken by an entire country! A beautiful country, with great mountains on which they both learned to ski. Both girls learned to read and write in French before English.

I learned that the game of squash was properly played with a soft ball, rather than with the hard ball that my IBM colleague in Chicago, Ches Porter, used when introducing me to the game. As a tennis player I took an immediate liking to squash. The ball stayed in play, the workout was intense. The hardball used in America made the game a version of racket ball with longer rackets. I did experience one near death experience on the squash court when Ches' racket slipped from his hand and caught me in the eye. Not flush in the eye, thankfully, but close enough for the swelling to close it, and convince me to play with glasses from that day on.

In Chicago Ches and I would play after work at the health club across the street from the IBM building on the Chicago River. I didn't play much while in New York but stepped into the big leagues in Paris. The IBM tower had two courts on the 40th floor, squash players from all over the world and a ladder that posted rankings. Brits and South Africans occupied the top of the ladder. All played with the soft ball which opens up the possibility of "drop shots", a dimension of the game unknown to me when I arrived.

Much of the play was during lunch. We were all staffers of one sort or another. I was a staffer at European headquarters early in his career. Many staffers were former heads of IBM in their respective countries, being routed through EHQ as part of their journey up the executive ladder. A staffers job is less exciting (certainly for those at the bottom of the staff ladder not involved in high stakes negotiations and politics) than sales. My squash games were often the highlights of my week. I advanced up the ladder to the number 4 spot at the end of my three-year assignment while giving those above me memorable matches. I met executives on the squash court I had little contact with during the rest of the day. It was best not to schedule a game before an important presentation to executives because it took several hours to cool down from a great 45-minute workout. Cooling off was best managed in the cafeteria during a leisurely lunch, paid for with committe d'enterprise coupons.

    Staff work in headquarters, in Paris, is not a bad gig as long as it lasts. Many try to extend, some manage to turn headquarter jobs into a career. That was not an option nor a goal for me. Wanting to continue the development of a skill set that had international dimension and with my career manager long gone from Chicago I landed back in the USA in Research Triangle Park, in the telecommunications division in another staff job. In North Carolina I met some upwardly mobile executives passing through the telecom division to enlarge their perspective (my purpose) but I was mostly among technologists who were in place for the long haul.

    Moving from a high rise overlooking Paris to a building in North Raleigh with no windows was a deflating "near death experience" from which I was looking to escape when I stumbled on the house at the top of the Vallejo Street steps in San Francisco that changed my life. I had excellent credit and some cash. I made an offer after seeing it in circumstances detailed in other "Bannana books". What I didn't mention in those books is that the property on the market consisted of four units, two in the front house I ended up buying, and a second in the back, occupied by a tenant. I was so struck by the place that I made an offer on the entire package. It was accepted. (The property had been on the market for over a year, as an estate sale. Buying a property in San Francisco occupied by a tenant is a formula for disaster, which I did not appreciate.)

    After considering the financial situation I had placed my family in I flew back to San Francisco and announced that I would have to back out of the deal, even if it involved losing my deposit. The only other option was for the estate to agree to separate the back property from the sale. I could then buy only the front property. The executor of the estate agreed, thereby granting me relief from my first financial near death experience. The fact I was leaving my source of income, IBM, at the moment I was encumbering myself with the greatest indebtedness of my life did not concern me. Things would work out, I was sure. (I was doing all this without having heard anything from Steve Jobs.)

    I started taking the house apart without suffering any near death experiences from my use of the crowbar and swings of a heavy hammer. Breathing in the fumes of paint and building materials that probably included lead and asbestos was certainly not good for me, but of little concern. I sometimes walked down the hill to buy a sandwich at Molinari's or a coffee at Cafe Trieste looking like a ghost.

    My second near death financial experience occurred when my family came out to join me and decided they could not stay, forcing a return to North Carolina by the family and initiating a desperate attempt on my part to put a half-finished house on the market. I was rescued by tenants who occupied the place for six years, paying a high enough rent to pay the mortgage until Dominique and I could return when Sofia, our youngest daughter, went to Carolina to join her sister Kristine. The real estate market in San Francisco was exploding. Middlemen kept calling me and asking if I needed money. They were ready to provide second mortgages based on the increasing value of the property. I needed the funds to both finance my Russian activities and continue renovation of the house, which included the building of a roof garden with a sauna.

    I kept borrowing, and traveling to and inside Russia, developing expertise, earning trust, and financing patents. Having experienced two near death experiences I finally sold the house in 2009, months before the collapse of the real estate bubble and moved to France. If I had not sold the house when I had to I would have suffered certain financial death. I had thus survived a third financial near death experience.

French medicine

In Paris the state of my health was dramatically improved, thanks to the medical system I had access to, via my French wife, Dominique, and the initiative of Sofia, my youngest daughter. My San Francisco friend Dennis also played a role. One of my last acts before leaving San Francisco, having sold my house, was to visit a dermatologist recommended by Dennis. He noticed a small mole just to the left of my nose that I was ignoring and suggested I have it checked out.

I did. The news was not good. The biopsy showed signs of cancer. There was no urgency according to the doctor but the situation required my attention once I got resettled in France. Dominique and I stayed for a few weeks in Grace, in southern France, with her mother and stepfather, before locating an apartment in Paris that we moved into. Once in Paris I asked around for hospitals specializing in skin treatments and learned that the hospital just down the street from Notre Dame had such specialty. I found my way there showed the staff the report I had received from the US and they agreed that my mole should be removed.

An appointment was made for the following week. I arrived, and the procedure was done in less than an hour. My doctor quizzed me about my medical status. I explained that I had recently moved to France that I had no insurance and that my wife was French. This should qualify me for a Carte Vitale, the key to the French medical system, I was told. I had to go to the administrative office of the 15th arrondissement where we were living with the appropriate documents. I followed this advice, found the office in a long grey structure being prepared for demolition, provided documentation on myself, and Dominique, and was told that my Carte Vitale would arrive in a month's time.

I got the Carte Vitale too late for it to cover the charge for my nose job, but it got me thinking about my left hip. My right hip had been replaced in San Francisco while I was in the Kaiser system. That injury was related to the ACL tear in my right knee that I neglected for too long. The doctor who operated on my right hip told me that my left side would require attention "before too long". Once the Carte Vitale arrived I figured it might be a good time to investigate how the French system compared with what I had experienced in America.

Sofia, my youngest daughter, played a key role in my next steps as she has on numerous occasions in my life. She was living in Paris in an apartment in a different part of town from the one Dominique and I were occupying, having graduated from Carolina. A piece of advice that I gave both my daughters when they graduated from college repeated advice Rose had given me when I graduated from Stanford (which led me to the Philippines). Do something at this point in life that you will never do again. It is a time for maximum exploration.

Put off climbing the corporate ladder. Follow your heart, your curiosity, your instinct. (In retrospect, this advice was similar to what Steve Jobs communicated in his Stanford talk.) Sofia left for Paris upon graduation to explore the city her mother had grown up in. Her linguistic abilities got her a job as a guide on the tour boats plying the Seine, the only person with an American passport ever hired, she was told. The job required fluency in five languages. (No problem for her, a native speaker of English, French, and Spanish, with fluency in German, Italian and Portuguese.)

In her spare time Sofia found a dance studio to her liking and was going there a couple of times a week. One day she suffered an accident that broke a finger in her left hand. I got a call from Dominique asking me to join her in the St. Antoine Hospital where I found Sofia lying in a hospital cot, preparing for an operation. She was pale and a little worried. All went well for Sofia at Saint-Antoine, a teaching hospital on rue de Faubourg in the 12th arrondissement, that day. She had to wear a cast on her hand for a while but otherwise her active life was unaffected.

Sofia noticed that Sainte-Antoine did hip replacements and mentioned this to me while offering to introduce me to some of the new friends she had made there. She accompanied me to the right department and spoke on my behalf (in perfect French) with two women who knew her.

"C'est mon papa." It's my dad.

They went through their list of available doctors and arranged an appointment for me with Dr. Levon Doursounian in a week. I was given a paper that confirmed my appointment. As I read it on the metro ride home I noticed that the letterhead of the hospital on which the appointment was confirmed included the names of all the doctors on the left hand side of the paper. I looked for Dr. Doursounian's name on that list. It was at the top. He was head of the department.

I took the metro to my appointment at the time indicated and was shown into an office where, in a few minutes, Dr. Doursounian arrived. He was wearing a red bow tie that stood out from his white coat, and round glasses, on a deeply tanned face with a broad smile. He asked me to lie on my back on the examination table, then remarked that my legs had slightly different lengths.

"Did I wear out one side of the heel on my right shoe?"
"Yes" how did he know?

I told him about the hip replacement done in the US, joking that I was doing a comparative study. He filled out some paperwork that I needed to get the X-rays he would need before the operation. He told me that an operation could be scheduled, but not for two months. I said this was not a problem. I was in no hurry. I asked him how much my hip replacement would cost. He said he did not know and directed me to an office near the exit of the hospital where my appointment would be made and my cost question would be answered.

I left that first meeting convinced I had made a great decision, guided by Sofia. I found the office Dr. Doursounian had mentioned, sat in the waiting area until the woman behind the computer was free, and approached her with my paperwork. A surgery date was confirmed.

"And how much is this going to cost?" I asked at the end of our meeting.

"Let's see a hip replacement, with an estimated six days in the hospital following, at 40 Euros a day, probably 250 euro" I was told. (I recalled going home from Kaiser two days after my operation.) I couldn't believe my good fortune as I contemplated an operation that would cost less than half of the monthly payment I had paid Kaiser in California. I would be able to compare not only the cost but the treatment given my right and left sides.

Several days before my operation, I visited Sainte-Antoine for my appointment with the anesthesiologist. I was told not to eat anything that morning. My blood would be drawn as part of the pre-operation examination. Giving blood, or having blood taken from me, is one of the least favorite processes that I have had to experience in my life. (I understand this near phobia is fairly common.) I explained this situation during my interview, conducted in French, to the anesthesiologist who was curious about the personal background that had contributed to my rather unique approach to her language.

My pronunciation is pretty good, since French was one of three languages I spoke as a child, but my grammar is spotty and my vocabulary is inventive. I told her my story: Czech mother, Finnish father, French as their common language, my immigration to America, my marriage to a French speaker. When it was time to take my blood I looked away, at the wall, focused on some images while I felt the sharp poke, and endured the rather lengthy time it took to fill several tubes.

I walked from her office to the waiting room down the hall where I would be delivered the results that I was to take with me. A few moments after sitting down I felt dizzy and heard the sounds of persons approaching me before passing out. When revived I explained that I had not eaten breakfast, felt queasy after the injection, and joked that I was thankful for fainting in a place where I was surrounded by so much medical expertise. When the results of my tests were given to me I was told the operation could go on. There was, however, a complication identified. My heart showed signs of arrhythmia, an irregular heartbeat. This would be addressed after my hip was replaced, I was told.

I checked into Sainte-Antoine the day before my operation was scheduled, into a room I shared with another patient. I was given equipment with which I was asked to shave all hair anywhere close to the area that would be operated on. The hospital's definition of this area far exceeded what I thought was relevant but I didn't raise any objection. (A precaution against infecting the operating room I was told later.) Early the next morning I was taken through the underground tunnel complex separating the building I was hospitalized in, by two handlers one at each end of my cot, to the operating room, which was very chilly.

I was the first patient of Dr. Doursounian on Monday morning. I recognized his eyes above the white mask covering his mouth and asked if he had had a good, restful weekend before losing consciousness to the anesthetic that had entered my blood stream. I woke up in the recovery area amid other patients and waited for my cot team to arrive and take me back through the underground labyrinth they were expert in navigating. The ride gave us a chance to swap political and sports opinions.

As the anesthetic wore off I started feeling the discomfort I remember from my first operation but it did not seem as painful. Was this a function of having had a previous exposure, or a qualitative difference, I had no idea. A nurse arrived and took me through menu options for lunch and dinner, which included three choices of appetizer, main course, cheese, and dessert. This was a clear differentiator from my Kaiser experience. I don't recall having *any* culinary choices in San Francisco.

This daily routine concerning menus developed into a nuanced discussion of cheeses, how main courses were cooked, recommended combinations of appetizer-entree choices that I developed with the young women who asked me these questions and entered my answers into a hand held device. I realized that, at 40 euro a day, I was making money by staying in the hospital, considering what meals cost on the outside.

Dr. Doursounian visited me the first evening after the operation with an X-ray that showed a clear difference between my hips. On my right hip a screw protruded from the artificial element that had been inserted into my hip into my bone, to insure its stability. On my left side the insert was so perfectly fitted into the remaining bone in my hip that no screw was needed. Dr. Doursounian did not make this point explicitly but was forced to agree with my analysis. I had been treated by an artist, a sculptor!

I learned later that Dr. Doursounian, born in Dakar, Senegal, had a cabinetmaker for a father and was inspired by the craftsmanship he observed in furniture production. He wanted to be an architect but there was no such degree available. Medical school diplomas were recognized in France and orthopedics most closely resembled his first love. In the days following the operation I was quite certain that I regained my ability to move my leg more quickly, and with less pain, than after my previous operation.

The student staff drew my blood, some with expertise, others more roughly. They all commented that my veins, as broad as "boulevards", that made their job easy. My heart was carefully monitored. My hospital stay was extended, without objection from me, to insure that I had the perfect dilution while background talks with the heart department took place. I was visited by physical therapists who enjoyed talking politics. The TV in my room (access to which cost me 3-euro a day) broadcast news of Jacque Chirac's triumphant visit to China, as head of a business delegation, first leader to be officially welcomed in Tiananmen Square. He proudly announced the signing of a big deal for Airbus, the European consortium building the alternative to Boeing in passenger jets. There was not much comment by French announcers on the part of the deal I found rather astonishing. The planes would all be "assembled" in China! Chirac appeared to essentially be giving the technology, funded to a large degree by European taxpayers, away to the Chinese, and providing Tiananmen Square, the location of the massacre of protesting students in 1989, international status, all in one brilliant move, as seen from the Chinese side at least. (I predict that the Chinese will announce domestic production of a plane remarkably similar to the Airbus, causing a near death experience to that industry in Europe.)

I started serious physical therapy on my own, walking up and down stairs between floors as soon as I was able. These walks through the facility showed me that many beds were empty. I came to the conclusion that St. Antoine was not being run as a business. It was a healing facility. As a patient in a teaching hospital I was often visited by groups of interns being shown around by an instructor. As a foreigner I was a curiosity. As someone ready to speak his mind, in the French language, my positive comments about the French system were very much appreciated. When it came time to leave I expressed genuine thanks to those who had filled my days with not only medical attention, but sincere friendship and good food.

Upon being discharged after a ten-day stay I was told I would get my bill mailed to me. I was instructed to walk to the heart department located in a different building in the Sainte Antoine complex. I began my relationship with that part of the teaching hospital by providing an initial electrocardiograph, which was explained to me, my unusual palpitations pointed out. In order to keep my blood properly diluted I was given a medication that I had to inject into my gut every day. (Dominique did this for me.) Each week I went to a facility down the street from where we were living to have my blood drawn. This routine kept my blood within the desired range but was a form of torture, given my stigma with injections.

My heart was thoroughly examined several times in a procedure that involved sending a camera down my throat, to provide a 360-degree perspective to a monitor I could see, while listening to experts and students discuss what they were seeing. It was decided that I should be subjected to "shock therapy", during which the heart is temporarily stopped and then restarted, hopefully with a regular beat. The day before that operation I had another appointment with the anesthesiologist, responsible for initiating my heart project. We joked about what she had gotten me into.

Anytime your heart is stopped there is reason to worry. When I went "under" in this procedure I admit to being more concerned than with the hip operation. The doctors explain that they can try up to three times during a procedure to restart the heart with a regular beat. In my case it took three shocks, I was told, after I resurfaced. I wore a monitor for a week following the procedure and was informed that my heart returned to its previous arrhythmic beat. The shock treatment was attempted a second time, with similar results.

"Would I be interested in receiving a pacemaker?"

If the French government was offering to install one I had no objection. And so it happened. As a result my trips through airport security are now complicated. Heart specialists in the US who have monitored the Medtronic device that was implanted remark at how seldom it appears to be needed, judging from the low power consumption. It has been toned down, as I understand, to reflect a passive, monitoring role. I left France a modern bionic man, with two artificial hips and a pacemaker. Paris made a positive contribution to my near death lifestyle without causing near death financial burdens.

Merci!

French medical know-how, and the system's willingness to apply it, may thus contribute to lengthening the days given me during which I may enjoy my grandchildren and continue connecting dots. Which brings me back to the central subject of this book, my time in Asia, experienced just after graduation from Stanford, during which I survived numerous near death (life affirming) experiences.

Martti Vallila

Impressions of Japan

This portion of the book is a journey back in time, thanks to letters discovered in Rose's home after her death. I have edited what I found providing *additional information and commentary in italics* tying the correspondence to themes of this book. I also include portions of a journal I kept during my time in the Philippines. My comments are informed by experiences in the world of hard knocks I entered upon my return to America.

When I left California in the spring of 1971 for Asia I cut short hair that had been allowed to grow (in the mountains) to a length Rose considered evidence of influences that had transformed, and not for the better, a son who had gone far away to collage. I felt a need to depart the culture I was in.

I had learned in anthropology classes how important the "right of passage" is in traditional societies, how the young males of a society are exiled from their communities and sent into "the wilderness" to return years later as men. Was I seeking transformation into adulthood by going to Asia? I suspected, when I boarded a JAL plane in San Francisco along with my VIA colleagues, that the days ahead would change my life. They did.

My first letter to Rose was written from Japan where the VIA group spent a week together before disbursing to various posts throughout Asia. It was written a few days after my arrival in Tokyo:

Letter 1 no date

We passed a post office on the way to the temple and the thought struck me- my promise of a post card. So here are the first words from the Orient. Traveling with the group is interesting. Our guide, Fugitisan, is a funny Japanese with a round belly who always has a good roar of a laugh and has been taking us on a train stop tour of temples and cities.

Japan seems filled with both, temples clinging to the bottoms of forested hills. Cities of small houses have taken over everything else. We spent a lot of our time in Tokyo and Osaka underground, in subways that are clean and efficient, and in stores, many of which have been built in huge underground complexes.

The Japanese have been great, although so far we've been restricted pretty much to the student crowd, which is trying hard to adapt to American customs. Japan is, I think, a confused society, seeking a sense of self amid the incredible hurry which here is a question of survival. My two days spent with a family were very special. A tiny house, two paper-walled rooms which change from bedrooms to living-dining rooms, a kitchen, and small bath, and one room on top, all very clean, and full of electrical gadgets.

My host family consisted of a son and his parents. At dinner the three men were served by the mother, who remained in the kitchen. The father did not speak much English but I got through to him when we started talking about fishing. After a while he went to a wooden drawer and pulled out a long thin paper on which he had preserved the tracings of some of the biggest fish he had caught! The small garden at the back of the house contained a pond full of goldfish. Just beyond the pond was a wooden fence on the other side of which was a train track on which we could hear the passing of trains.

As the honored quest I was given first turn in the small tub before dinner. The water was so hot that it took me many minutes to enter and achieve the sitting position. I suspected that my hosts were huddled on the other side of the paper wall separating the tub room from the all purpose room, speculating on how I would handle this custom, which was the closest I got to a near death experience during my week in Japan. I emerged red and hungry. My male hosts then followed me into the tub after I had cooled the water.

The mix of kids on the tour has turned out pretty well. All have a sense of adventure somewhere, and although some fit very neatly into the American abroad stereotype, that's not so obvious here, where the surroundings have more than a bit of America of their own. We have spent the last

Martti Vallila

two days in a religious city, (*Koyasan*) getting up at four to go chanting.

People here are very consciously members of a larger group, self disciplined. When they stand around it's in straight lines, in order, on command. Their cheerlessness reminds me of the military and karate exhibitions are a bit frightening. All of this with word that Japan is militarizing in self-defense. America is opposed by most of the students we have met but then we have been visiting the famous private universities.

I look back from here onto America as a land where things can be done, if there are ideas. We are reading some words here about the Daniel Ellsberg case.... An old Japanese professor told me the other day that America has "a strong enough tradition to survive" and he is hoping the same for Japan. Japan, the nation that spends much of its time forgetting its past and then feels the need to look somewhere for tradition.

During the three free days I think I'll go to Kyoto, or to the north, to find more countryside. Much of the air is cloudy, smoggy, and reminds of those Chinese paintings where the mountains gradually disappear into a cloudy distance. Tomorrow we talk to another group of students and go to a basketball game. There are two guitars in the group, plenty of songs, which take me back a couple of years to the coffee houses of the early anti-war movement.

Letter 2 sent on July 4, 1971

Today is Sunday the 4th of July, which makes me think back to 4ths of the past, to the dinner at Laperouse with Marja in Paris, to the baseball game last year in Alabama, to the 4th we spent in Athens, and to the many that we passed in America, either in Washington or at the beach, realizing, of course, that we didn't even discover the 4th until 1958. I will spend this 4th in Kyoto. Some of us have thought of going to the US consulate here, where there will undoubtedly be a party.

This morning I saw my first Americans here, when I went to change money. People in Kyoto, Osaka, Koyasan, Nara, our other stops, were almost entirely Japanese. This morning I set off for the Chinese department of Kyoto University, it is one of the best in the world, was going to go as a French student, asking about China, but then discovered it was Sunday, which means nothing to the stores, they are all open, closing instead, one day during the week, but Sunday does close the post office, schools and most offices.

I was interested in getting material on China for the Philippines because I had been told that one of the courses I would be teaching first semester at Mindanao State University would be the history of modern China.

We arrived here yesterday from Koyasan, perhaps the most religious spot in Japan, a wonderful collection of Buddhist temples set on a mountaintop, far removed from the city noise and dirt. I saw the monks, and those studying to be, enter a small room filled by brown candle light, and chant, in resonating voices, the proscribed words. Ancestral tablets filled the walls. The train ride to and from took us through forested hills being preserved. Only a few houses and rice terraces have carved this place. The track followed the decent of a stream whose path was blocked frequently to milk it for electrical energy.

There is much electrical energy here. Many houses have color television sets and mechanical gadgets that seem out of place among straw mats and paper walls. The Japanese themselves seem to have some sort of electrical energy running through them. Our guide until yesterday, Fujitasan, is a most unusual person, dedicated to introducing foreigners to Japan, and then giving them names of friends in various spots where we will settle. He has promised me a list when I am ready to travel through Asia.

Japan is a very large collection of little things. The exceptions: the huge department stores in Tokyo and the gigantic Buddhist, wooden, temples. Otherwise the big is made up of collections of the very small. The individual houses, apartments stacked on, and around, and between. There have been no big plans, rather, things have been allowed to collect.

I am beginning to understand the art of communication here, where the point made is more important than the process. In this I am of course handicapped, as I don't speak the language, but I enjoy most of all, perhaps, speaking in the language of gesture and laughter, where there are no precise words to push the point around there is only the art that people can do together.

I hope you spent this day on the beach. If so, hope you gave my best to all the beach people.

In two days we leave for Taipei, where I hope to swim, and we will make the transition from students to teachers, because the government of Taiwan will allow us to speak only with businessmen, not with students. Give my love to Marja and tell her to send me her address. I look forward to landing in Mindanao where my life as a tourist will end and I will have work as a regular part of all this.

There are not many western faces in the crowds here, even in Tokyo where I expected more. The hot baths are something that should spread from here. It's a daily tradition and puts one to sleep relaxed. I suppose that the reality of my situation hasn't dawned on me yet. I am still traveling around with a group of Americans, not knowing whether it's summer or fall, and what lies ahead in the coming two years.

The Japanese people are fantastic. Very honest in an unassuming way. They believe in many things, in rules, in numbers, in categories. Sometimes when I smile I am not sure it's understood. Today one boy asked me whether I was a "typical American". He noticed my slanted eyes, and I am once again acutely conscious of my background.

I want very badly to face a hard challenge and I think it's coming in two weeks. I took my first malaria pill last night, a week behind schedule. I think I will enjoy photography very much. I think I see that way anyway, and this will preserve images. (*I bought the first single lens reflex camera of my life in Hong Kong on this trip to begin what has become a life long hobby.*)

The people here sing on the way to work, they all wear black coats with lettering on the back. This is a land of pictures for me as the letters are but patterns. For me there are not many categories, distinctions, distractions. But for the Japanese, who read the characters, all of those things are strongly present. They live in a very real, cold, hard, logical way. To the American, who passes through, Japan can remain the mystic land. Ah, how things are the opposite of what they seem here.

The islands and jungles of the Philippines

Mindanao State University (MSU) was established by the Philippine government in the hills overlooking Lake Lanao, in the middle of a region inhabited by the Maranao people. It was given the mission of connecting the Christian and Islamic communities of the largest, and least developed, of the more than 7000 islands that constitute the Philippine nation. Half of the student body was Maranao, the rest Christian, all on scholarship. The Maranao students came from "ghost schools" surrounding the lake. Schools for which funds had been sent from Manila, but were not built (like the paved road that existed on maps in Manila but not on the ground). The Christian students were bright scholarship winners from "feeder" schools in the lowlands of Mindanao and surrounding islands.

The Maranao were converted to Islam centuries ago. It is more accurate to say that Islam was adapted and integrated by the Maranao into their native belief system. Maranao land was never occupied by the Spaniards who introduced Christianity to the Philippine Islands after Magellan "discovered" them, in 1521, arriving in Cebu where he was killed by chief Lapu Lapu. By 1971 Islamic influence in the Philippines was limited to the southern islands of the Sulu Archipelago and the interior of Mindanao. The Moslems had a reputation as fierce fighters, defenders of their land. Generals Pershing and Wood served in the Philippines, in Mindanao, and the invention of the Colt 45 artillery SAA revolver (to replace the 38 caliber Colt M) was attributed to the need to have a handgun powerful enough to repel a charging Moslem "juramentado" equipped with a sword, dressed in white, on a suicide mission.

I was recruited to become a two-year replacement faculty member of the social sciences department, placed there by Stanford's Volunteers in Asia program. Replacements were needed to fill in for faculty receiving additional training. The VIA placement accomplished something very rare. It provided volunteers with local status, as teachers. The Philippines received more Peace Corps volunteers than any other country but these volunteers were often dropped into villages with little guidance from above, and no place in the local society. The best ones figured out what to do once they got there, which was often very different from their stated mission.

Peace Corps volunteers were paid by the US government and had a dollar kitty awaiting them at the end of their assignments. We drew local salaries of 400 pesos a month, which converted into $60, just enough to live in the local economy. Housing was provided at no cost.

Dwight Clark founded VIA. His genius was to have built VIA from the "bottom up", starting by providing native speakers of English to Hong Kong's rooftop schools and expanding from there, at the invitation and initiative of the host countries, to filling two-year posts. Asian society is highly structured. People need to understand where you fit in. This determines how you are treated. The teacher is a highly respected person and expected to talk during a class, while the students listen.

This one-way communication was something I was not prepared for and attempted to change within the confines of my classroom. The other VIA volunteers at MSU taught English, for which they were qualified. I was asked to teach a rather wide range of subjects requiring a replacement teacher. Most challenging, for me, was the history of China course. I had taken a modern Chinese history course at Stanford (thank goodness) and an anthropology course on the Chinese family. I stocked up on material (including some red books) at the second floor of the huge store in Hong Kong selling ivory and propaganda, which I managed to carry in my luggage through Taipei.

I later buried this material in the compost pit behind our cottage when Marcos declared martial law in late 1972, using as justification the "Maoist insurrection" occurring in Luzon and Mindanao. His martial law declaration closed

MSU and brought an early end to my assignment. The timing was OK with me. I was sick with hepatitis, acquired from a "sterilized" needle with which I had been given a booster shot of gamma globulin at MSU's "health center".

I encountered many "near death" experiences during my eighteen months in the Philippines. I will take the reader through them via the letters I sent to Rose in which I make casual reference to events that, when seen from a distance, seem more dangerous than they were, or appeared to me to be at the time.

I have *added detail in script* where it is appropriate. My aim is to provide the reader with an account written mostly in real time.

Letter 1 July 14

I am writing these first impressions from Mindanao with my new pen of Chinese manufacture, which I bought in Hong Kong, figuring that if this is the start of some sort of Asian experience what better tool to record it with than one made "in China", the real China.

Also found out the courses I will be teaching this first semester: Chinese history and geography of the world, which in my mind is an anthropology course. (*This course turned out to be a real geography course, once I found proper text books in the library.*) Will find out tomorrow about days, times, and the rest of the particulars. Met some other volunteers here through a couple of British fellows and some Stanford guys- good crowd I think. One of the girls that came down with us has my interest.

We can see Lake Lanao below. I heard tales of a motor boat which I hear prompted another volunteer to build a pair of water skis, so maybe...the room I have now with Jay, another two year volunteer, is 8 feet by 12 feet with two beds, two cupboards, and 4 pillows. That's about it, but we hope to move into a cabin, hut, soon, like the one we visited this evening.

Few chances to meet people. Arrived on a 3am plane from Manila, after 2 days there, and slept as soon as I arrived. Lots of crickets at night, and in a full moon the place looks great. There is an old tennis court and some Filipinos are apparently pretty good. My twenty hours in Hong Kong command me to return to that place. Most cosmopolitan city so far, without question. The humidity is very high. Junks sail in the bay next to huge international steamers, and each day requires several crossings of the bay on, the Star ferry. Hong Kong is a most mysterious place, orientals, westerners, good prices, and a bustling pace. Downtown could be anywhere, except the signs speak of Asia. I was talked into buying a silk shirt while window shopping at the communist propaganda shop *(by a man who approached me and started measuring me on the sidewalk. When I explained that I was leaving for the Philippines in the morning he took me inside and offered me a cold San Miguel beer. I decided I would buy something and settled on a silk shirt which proved very useful in the humid Philippines.*

The town has everything and gave me a taste of what I imagine in Singapore and Thailand. For now it's this island with its quiet scenery. Today the clouds drooped over the hills on the other side of the lake. We got a tour during the 2 1/2 hour drive from the airport through the small towns that dot the coast. Water buffalo and goats calmly munched on the side of the paved road, knowing instinctively, just how far they need to move to avoid our honking jeep.

Not much surf, but the ocean looked enticing and I think a party is set for this weekend, so I'll get my first ocean swim. We are not exactly experiencing the old colonial luxuries. It's a tough life in this small room and obvious that the most important element here is people. They find comfort in company, I think.

Manila is a "funky" city, lots of noise and brightly colored jeepneys and shirts. We changed money at "black market" rates in the middle of the post office. Went to the

Martti Vallila

embassy, unfortunately the ambassador was down with a cold and I talked instead to a couple of other fellows who briefed me, and assured me that I will know more than they about the situation in a couple of weeks. Told me to drop by next time up, which will be during vacation, I guess.

    I don't know much about the situation here yet. The weather, which is warm in the morning, a six o'clock sunrise, and rain at sunset at seven that signals the end of the day, except to the guitars which begin to play throughout the campus. I have not bought mine yet because I am waiting for a weekend trip to an island where they are made. My suit, which is now getting a bit dirty, has held up well, and is due for a rest in the closet. I will send word about books I might need once I find out exactly what the classes will be and how much they have here. The first couple of weeks I will manage with the stuff I brought, and old notebooks.

    I am getting excited by the prospect of the classroom, and will spend the next couple of weeks exploring the surroundings. There is another anthropologist here who is supposed to be very interesting. All in all the scene reminds me of the Spanish coast, with crickets at night, a solitude, the panorama, coconut trees, and very far from American thoughts, which creep up only occasionally now to haunt, questions of purpose, of justification, of goals. I think people have been living this way for many years and have managed to make it work.

    Please number your letters so I get an idea of what I am getting. This is No. 1 and will be mailed, I hope, on the 15th to give you some idea of how long it takes to cross our worlds. (*The letter arrived in Washington DC on August 15th.*)

First journal entry from the Philippines describing a "near death experience", my first class

I've found a leisurely moment now, where I suspect I'll find many more, in the school building the only part of my life here that runs according to an exterior schedule, and unlike in the lands of schedules (the US and Japan) who run and depend on them, here schedules are still considered exterior structures, no more than that.

On Friday I was running to my first class. I was running down the path to the social sciences building when I passed some students who asked, "What is the matter, sir?" I explained that I was late for class, late for MY class.

"Oh, no need to worry sir", they replied coaxing me to walk. Sure enough the minute delay seemed to have no effect on the students who had gathered outside the classroom now for 20 minutes, but seemed not at all surprised or chagrined when I walked up, carrying a crumpled raincoat and my notebook.

They took their places and I was suddenly faced with a podium in front, about 10 faces looking forward, a filled blackboard, no chalk, and absolutely no plan. My first instinct was to tell them my name. I then tried to write it on the board, fumbled around for a bit of chalk, found some chalk in a crack, and then began erasing a spot on the board with my hand.

One of the girls gently offered, "here sir, you can use this", gave me her Kleenex. I wasn't sure if I was operating with a subconscious desire to make them laugh but I needed a reaction, some kind of reaction. The girls in the middle three seats giggled.

OK Now down to business. "Now that you know my name, maybe I should get around to asking yours...I won't remember them the first time, so you must be patient."

"Here sir, take these", one of the boys handed me his class card. Well now that's a step in the right direction. Class cards, this place has class cards. This must be a class, and the scatterbrain at the head of the room, the only one left standing, ME, is the teacher!

So I took up their class cards and my intuition about names led me to another thought. "I still want you to put your names on a piece of paper and then under that I want you to tell me what history or geography courses you have had before."

A stroke of genius, I thought. Have them writing. I'll find out something and the five minutes will give me a chance to compose myself.

There were questions. "What kind of history? What's that again, sir?"

"Oh, world history, Asian history (tell me anything, doesn't matter, anything at all, was in my thinking, but that's not the language of school, of fact, of specifics).

"I want to know courses that are like what this is about to be." And then another thought, from my anthropological roots, "and on the other side, I want you to put where you were born and where you have travelled."

They were actually doing it, heads bent to the paper, pausing. There was quiet. I understood the power of the teacher. Ask them to do anything, to write, fill up space, be quiet when I speak. What an enticement to one who has suffered the injustices of the other side, has wasted hours reading assignments concocted by old maids, hungry for power.

Well, I have resolved not to fall into this trap, all too easy in this land of "sirs". I needed to know their schedules, when they could not meet. I carved out some more room on the board. By this time chalk was getting on my clothes and I felt at home. Made a list of potential class times, asked each student what was possible for them, made a joke with one of the girls who was free no other time: "you are always busy!"

Need I say I was rolling. Secretly I knew all along that things would turn out, and I hold out the same thought today, just before the start of really serious classes....

Letter 3 (2 is missing) **July 24**

Only the kindness of my heart and warm memories and the many things you have done for me in my past 21 years prompts this letter, my third! Without any word from you. The only possible explanation, besides maternal negligence, is the postal service. I am not abandoning hope all together.

Let me take one last precaution. If this is the last letter to reach you before August 25th, (my birthday) let me say now, on July 24th, that I will think of you then.

We just got back from a weekend on the west of the island which we reached in a jeep on rocky roads, about a five hour drive, through wild country controlled sometimes by rebels but most of the time by local people who simply have their own interest in mind and stop passing cars to sell them crabs which are caught in the bay.

Back to play a game of Sunday tennis on the one court, to plan lessons for this Tuesday. (My tennis opponents were locals, and occasionally, Ross Flynn, the wife of the British couple. The local men were astonished to see a large, powerful, scantily dressed woman whacking a tennis ball. I was astonished at some of the things I saw pass bye as we play, considered perfectly normal by the locals. For example, one day two men walked through the court carrying a live monkey tied on a stick. I presumed the monkey had been recently captured, and could not imagine what was going to happen to it next.

The site was so much a part of the place that it did not attract the attention of anyone. I thought at the time that if I were ever to write about how different a world Marawi City was, the image of a wild monkey on a stick being considered perfectly ordinary would make the point.)

Am at a dinner at a cottage where I am listening to Armed Forces Radio telling me the world news, which seems far removed. Here the days follow in a quiet pace, with even the prospect of a civil war, it is a very quiet scene.

It's difficult to think of things in their large context. The sun rises at six, sets at seven, and in between, people try to manage.

Pagadian, where we went this weekend, had a large early morning market, which all the small farmers attend. It also had dance halls, the first I have seen in the Philippines, where they sing only love songs. Love songs explain a great deal here. Love, pure and simple, is the core.

The Philippines is mostly a young land where the background music is teenage. The community here has made me feel very much at home, as part of the tennis and basketball communities, and as part of the faculty. I have gone to several houses for dinner, and am beginning to appreciate Philippine hospitality. The kindness of the girls here.

The university is on a hill, removed, much like Stanford, from the adjacent community. In the coming weekends I hope to journey around to the Marawi City market, among the people with their children everywhere. A lot of free time to spend at cockfights, gambling, or just sleeping in one corner, or another.

I feel very much a part of a developing wave, especially among the Moslems who are just now getting organized, and their leaders will emerge from our students. Teaching here is difficult because I can never be sure what the kids know. About the world map, for instance, and how much of the indifference comes from poorly done preparation.

A couple of kids hijacked a plane to Beijing some months ago, so interest in China is up, but it's really a situation where I can take little for granted.

This weekend we visited the house of one of my students, a wooden shack held by stilts above a yard with chickens and pigs, fourteen brothers and sisters. I realized what a step the university and its premises must be from there. There is running water (cold) at the university for at least two hours a day. This student is making a jump from day to day in a barrio to her first glimpse of the world.

This is why I am confused. Should I explain the continents, the countries, or more sophisticated ideas of climate, geography?

I am learning much, I think, about a part of the world, which is in the papers, and top, as the British say.

This letter is being mailed in Manila so hopefully it will get through. When it does, please send word back, about the number you have already received. Hope Washington treats you well. Love to my friends. Give them good news, from the tropics, where each day is still an adventure. (*Letter arrived on August 7.*)

Letter 4 mailed August 2

I just got your letters, which have been sitting in the mailbox in Iligan City for several days, uncollected and your telegram, which I decided not to answer, feeling certain that one of my letters would reach you soon.

Let me describe my setting, for as I remember, my previous letters have been filled with impressions and sketches, but lack a larger picture, which during the first few days had not yet taken shape.

It is now the third week, my life is settled a bit. I am teaching three classes, sociology, to first and second year students. This class is a lot of fun. I have some characters in it. Girls sit up front, boys in the back, and they have overcome initial shyness so that they now laugh when I am funny. I am teaching the course from two books, injecting some worldly comments.

About 25 kids, and more keep transferring in. I suspect the class is getting a good reputation.

The geography of the world class, also on Tuesdays and Thursdays, has been more difficult. It's smaller, about 10, and I was immediately faced by problems deciding what the kids know, about the globe, for instance, deciding on a lecture strategy for the course. I finally found a book in the library, but no textbooks for the students.

This has made me aware of the difficulty of teaching to students with a different background, and explaining to them why weather changes in different latitudes when all they have ever seen is the same day over and over again. The kids are older, mostly history majors, and sharp.

The most difficult course to organize has been Chinese history. It is listed on the schedule as history of China from western opening to the overthrow of the republic, which I suppose they think happened in 1949. Well, that's not what I intend to teach, nor what the students are interested to learn.

One of the campus legends is the story of the three students who hijacked a plane to Beijing four months ago, and used the same map I am working with! There are five students enrolled. We meet Tuesday evenings for two hours and discuss readings, most of which will come from the books I brought (having purchased them in the propaganda store in Hong Kong, and smuggled them through Taiwan).

The books will have to be passed around but will at least have more currency about events in China than what is available in the library here, where the only modern Chinese book is the tirade of a defeated Nationalist general. So far we have just done ancient China, so I can't say yet how the red breeze will be received, but I have a hunch it will be popular, and suddenly legitimized by Nixon, and his puppet Marcos, who has been forced to "the reality of recognition".

The library was extremely limited. There were often just two copies of a text book, one for the teacher, and the other for students to sign out, in turn. The teacher in Asia is expected to fill class time with lecture. This is particularly challenging to someone asked to teach subjects outside their area of expertise.

My method was to try to draw the students out, into discussion, by asking questions. A particularly memorable sequence in my Chinese class, when I was trying to illustrate the point that Chinese has many spoken dialects, but is written with a single set of hieroglyphics, was to ask: "so if a Chinaman from the north met someone from the south, how would they communicate?"

To this, many raised their hands. The unanimous answer: "In English!"

My students were applying their circumstances to my question. There are more than 70 different languages spoken in the Philippine Islands. The common language for all, the medium of instruction, is English. There was a movement to make Tagalog the national language and medium of instruction when I was there.

In my opinion, facility in English is a comparative advantage for the Philippines, in the global economy, allowing for call centers, similar to those that initially tied India to the international marketplace.

Another area of adjustment upon arrival was the size of meals. In the beginning I served myself multiple cups of rice and numerous servings of sardines and vegetables, in the school cafeteria. Over time my metabolism slowed down, and I was satisfied consuming much smaller portions.

There was no phone service so it was necessary to walk somewhere hoping to find the person in their office, or at home, at an expected time. Electricity was very limited. Most homes did not have it. The pace of life was dictated by the sun.

I have joined both the tennis and basketball communities. Am on the faculty basketball team, so there is time and opportunity for exercise, which begins here at sunrise at 6 which is when the basketball team practices.

A small community of young teachers has taken us in, usually beach parties on weekends and lots of formal occasions.

Took a trip last weekend with the vice president of external affairs to some extension high schools in the west of the island. Saw some more towns and got to know his secretary, Betty, probably the prettiest, in my eyes, of the many kind Filipino girls. She manages to have her friends bring coconuts up to the school frequently, and we eat them at our parties. Coconut meat, mixed with juice and sugar. She promises to teach me some of the local dialect.

I have gotten some film developed. No results yet, because electricity has gone bad in the town, and the studio lacks printing paper, but hopefully I will have something to send soon.

The sense of personal space or distance was almost nonexistent, particularly among the young. As I picked up slides at the photo shop in Iligan, and sat on a bench to view them, I was immediately surrounded by youngsters squeezing for a look. I learned not to open anything on the street that I was not prepared to share with anyone around.

My visits to the market in Marawi were also instructive. Stands specialized in individual items, like bananas. The bananas sold in the Philippines are much smaller then those found in the west. And much tastier!

Early in my stay I asked the banana vendor to pick out a bunch for me. Taking them home, I found that bunch unusually sour. From then on, I picked my bunches myself, figuring that the seller had used my invitation to unload product that it would have been difficult to unload on someone who knew his bananas.

We look at the lake below, which I have not yet tapped for skiing, although I have heard about two boats used by a research group studying the lake. Gorgeous sunrises and sunsets frame the day.

The anthropologist here is an exciting, enthusiastic, vigorous man, just returned from the States. He has discovered native art, which demonstrates precious craftsmanship and will probably participate in a study of the industrialization of Iligan City. I've met him and intend to talk about future projects. Trips to some local tribes are also promised.

I don't know how much anthropology work I'll be able to do these first couple of months with my heavy schedule of preparations. My intentions are first to achieve a comfortable position within the community. Baradas, the anthropologist, suggests that I look in Marawi City for a place to live if I really want to study the people, and I think there is a strong chance of this second semester, especially if I face the prospect of staying in my small room, brightened only recently by a print from Marja, and a straw hat.

Rest assured that I am alive, eating well, feeling healthy, working hard, and enjoying the whole thing very much. There are plans in the works to spend Christmas in Indonesia, if we can get the proper papers, so I might even

Martti Vallila

get to cross the equator before the year runs out. (*Letter arrived August 10.*)

Letter 5 August 7

I went to the post office a couple of days ago where I found two letters (2nd & 3rd) along with a collection of hurried telegrams. May your worries be laid to rest. Looks as if 10 days separate us, on average.

And contrary to the memories of old inhabitants, and rumors that sway through Washington, things are quite peaceful here. This weekend was a good example. On Saturday I went down to Iligan as a member of the faculty basketball team (as center). We played a local college and lost by two points.

The truck taking us back to MSU did not come until after dinner, so we ate at a Chinese restaurant. There were a lot of Muslims there. We then went bowling. They don't have automatic pin-setters, some legs appear and kick the knocked ones away.
The pins are reset by hand.

Today a group went back to the beach. I don't mean to sound as if the place is a country club, although the 9 hole golf course which is the first thing one notices driving up the hill to MSU does not exactly speak of the university's task of uplifting the local population, or maybe it does, to the American standard.

I give my first tests this week, and will find out at least if students understand my English. I have been thinking seriously about moving in with a family in order to get a glimpse of life here, and several have been suggested. Should know by the end of the week.

For transportation, the university has offered me a horse, which I saw for the first time yesterday. Has a big, sagging belly. Haven't tried to ride it yet, as every time I approach, she either turns her rear to prepare a kick or tries to bite me. She's already grabbed my shirt. So I don't know about that idea.

Chris, the British volunteer, has ridden her and says she's slow. And I have to find a place to keep her, and time in which to care. So far, contrary to expectations, my life has not slowed down, because I am still preparing my work, to the amusement of many.

A visiting sociologist from Smith of all places (*the college my sister Marja attended*) passed by. She said you still have to be a junior in good standing to marry. Dwight Clark, head of the VIA program, also dropped bye for a couple of days and left a short wave radio which brings us radio Beijing, France, en francais, and the US, a good mix.

It looks as if I'll spend my birthday on the island of Negros, just to the north, where the faculty basketball team has been invited to help celebrate their foundation day. I'll try to pass bye Cebu and get a guitar on the way back.

The local elections are soon approaching, and could provide excellent material for a couple of articles. I have met some people who may give me an unusual perspective on them. The big issue at present is a proposal to drop the level of the lake 10 meters, which would put Marawi City more than 1/2-mile inland. A student will do a paper on this, I hope.

All decisions are made by a few who have access to information and power while most spend their days around the bamboo home, looking out their window as we pass bye by car. The caribou do most of the work, huge animals led by men holding a string that ends in a ring in their nose.

Tonight, Shelley, another of the volunteers, cooked us all dinner in a cottage. The rum here is cheap and good. Same with the beer, San Miguel, which you should try. A lot is exported to the US.

Finally, I hope that short silences don't begin to cause you worries. I have found nothing here to argue against the natural goodness of man. On the contrary, I think the Filipinos probably know more about this than anyone else.

I can just imagine the heat of August in Washington, heard a description of it on the radio. Think about starting a book. I want something to work on when I get back.
(*Letter arrived August 19.*)

proposal to drop the lake 10 meters and put Marawi City 1/2 mile inland. This is good Zodiac country, if people would begin to use larger boats.

This is probably the last letter you'll get before my birthday. I will be thinking of the family, probably on the island of Negros, where we have a basketball game. Joining the team has introduced me to another bunch of very interesting people. It's going to be impossible passing the 25th without thinking of past years. Hope you have a chance to spend it well, with friends. Cook a cake they'll really enjoy. Love from your 22 year old number 1 son.
(*Letter arrived August 24.*)

Martti Vallila

Journal entry from the "week of the Friday 13th massacre"

    Well, I suppose we are in the middle of what you'd call a crisis *(or "near death experience)*, an impression anyone would get from passing the girl's dorm where they've been staying up late, crying. Some have decided to leave for home, fearing a Moslem massacre on Friday 13th (40 days after a massacre of Moslems in Cotobato). The rumor began with a pronouncement from "the spirit of the bottle", but has been spread and accepted with a speed that suggests greater influences.
    Some are undoubtedly coincidence. President Tamano is away, Marcos is due on Thursday, some girls saw a man with a mask and gun last Saturday. Moslem girls have been sleeping in Marawi City and some have warned their friends to be careful.
    This morning a note appeared on campus that I did not have a chance to see but apparently suggested that the time for revolution has come. My own suspicions are that this incident holds important clues that religious fears are being played upon by people interested in conflict, for its various rewards.
    The Moslem administration, in its convocation, took great pains to convince that the rumor was unjustified. Baradas spoke of the anthropological differences between the Maranao of our region and the Magindanao of Cotobato, explaining why the Moslems here would not massacre. They are the majority, well organized, with an internal legal system, and have not had the "land grabbing" problem. But he seemed less than certain himself, or maybe left this impression because his academic posture makes him less assertive than the politicians.
    The mayor of Marawi promised his city was so safe he didn't even carry a gun, then walked out with a pistol bulging from his pocket. A lawyer who claimed to have the confidence of the Moslems of Cotobato promised they had

no intention of killing anyone at MSU (it is against their religion). Now, if they want to go back to the south, he'll help them with money and bullets, for revenge, if not with men....

The university seemed determined to play down the crisis, and decided not to call in troops, unless asked to, explicitly, by a student vote. They will rely first on the Marawi police, that the Christians don't trust. The mayor's reputation doesn't hold water. He has swindled during a trip to Mecca and his gang was allegedly responsible for stealing some cattle from MSU.

The students want legitimate outside protection by non-Moslems, of Christians. Their fears seem genuine. But it appears to me that sending troops would escalate the situation in the eyes of the president, of Manila, of the locals, and play into the hands of anyone with a stake in disorder. (Anyone from an American campus finds it hard to believe that calling troops from the outside will calm things down.)

No one spoke of anything beyond the concrete situation. The "revolution" was only hinted at. The first speaker talked about the whispering game. Another speculated about what drunken soldiers might do. Students spoke of their fears.

The administration (Moslem dominated) certainly has a stake in its success, with its mission of uplifting the minorities. But the Moslems must, at the same time, be very conscious of the power that lies in their ethnicity, in their separation, independence. I believe the smart ones can ride the fence for a long time, but eventually, local interests will prevail.

If a strong enough base of support for the university is built in the community, which sees MSU as a government imposition, this base can be appealed to, in the end. That appeal may, however, unleash a power that will grow beyond the control of its origins (the wealthy Moslems). The outcome probably depends on how big the payoff is from Manila, and how powerful are the opposing local forces.

The students have a stake in education here, particularly the locals, I think, but at the same time, the revolutionaries must destroy vehicles of integration, such as MSU. Christ, what a mess.

I ate pie with Miromar who explained the Moslem custom of Ramadan, which comes once a year, in October. It is forbidden to even swallow saliva during the day. Classes are disrupted because pupils are always running to windows, to spit. He promised to take me to small villages during that time.

He also assured me of peace. It's against his religion to kill even insects, except for food or revenge. However, the possibility of hostages still exists.

Six city policemen are on campus, to assure students. The "most experienced" men. No interruption of classes. Students are allowed to leave till the 15th but beyond that those with scholarships will lose them, and their dorm spaces will be given to others.

Letter 7 August 25

    This is my birthday letter, because today is my birthday and right now I am taking a happy birthday Philippine after lunch siesta. People do this on days other than birthdays as well. But today being my birthday, because it falls on a multiple of 365 1/4 days from the day I arrived on, makes this nap special, just as it made breakfast, an otherwise ordinary meal, special, although I did have some trouble getting up for it.
    Last night the basketball ream drank a lot of rum. I think our opponents are trying to defeat us with liquor, and I played the harmonica to local songs, after singing a foreign one of my choosing...I count to ten in Finnish in a deep voice, while strumming the guitar. Just when I went to bed, really needing to, my teammates came in singing happy birthday and gave me a box with a frog and three snails inside. I have been researching local mythology on the items since.
    My birthday will make the game tonight and the meal afterwards, followed by a nude night swim, very special. Having a birthday just provides an excuse for considering some of the very special things that happen all the time.
    Yesterday Marcos suspended the writ of habeas corpus. I suppose that's what you read about in the States. Try as I have, today I spent a good bit of the morning in the paper, I have not managed to understand the relevance of what all those bastards in Manila are doing to our visit here, to the lives of most people here, in Panagueti, on the island of Negros, known as the "town of gentle people".
    We arrived last night on a PAM boat that we took from another island that we were able to reach with a big boat from Iligan. The two boat rides were connected by an 18km jungle trip in a jeep with a broken axel at three in the morning, which is the best time to see the jungle.
    The first boat reminded me of the Majorca trip. Just add chickens, squealing pigs on the first deck, fresh mangoes,

the best of many local fruits, and local customs that enable 13 to sleep in 9 bunks. People who have grown up in families of ten are, I suppose, accustomed to using another's body as a pillow. In the boys dorm at MSU some rooms have 7 or 8 inside.

The second boat ride in the small put-put motor powered PAM boat at sunrise was picture-taking time. I intend to send the already exposed and developed black and white reels to the States with a friend who'll send them to you. I want Marja to make contact sheets, and then develop, enlarge and print those she likes. I'll also send at least one roll of color slides that should be developed there. Developing has been pre-paid.

They should get to you in a couple of weeks and give you a better glimpse of things here than I can possibly do in words. From here I will leave the others, who are rushing back to MSU, and go to Cebu to buy a guitar. Next week is founder's week at MSU, so it's full of celebration and classes are suspended till Thursday.

People here enjoy celebrations, know how to celebrate. Elton, a classic American, said it best: "I've been to more parties here in a month than in my four years in college"!

The Filipinos are getting a big kick out of him. He is the other foreigner on the basketball team, and he sure is fun to watch, with his super competitive attitude. *The Filipinos play a very fluid game. When I go in, it is as center, as I am the tallest member of the team. In the US I never played much basketball, because I was considered too short.*

Just before I left MSU I got a letter from the American embassy, which had your birthday kiss inside. I have gotten one letter from Marja so far, and I think the mail is moving regularly. These are troubled times, so the papers say, so who can tell. Trouble always seems to be BETWEEN places, never in them.

Send me dedechek's *(grandfather's)* address. I will send him a post card with a pretty girl on it. Also tata's *(father's)* if you have it around. Did he send anything for birthday?

It's about two o'clock here now, so I suppose you've just begun celebrating, and we certainly have not finished. I think we pledged to out-do the 5 bottles of rum last night, and I am suspicious of an ice cream surprise as well.

Hope you had more than memories on this day. I imagined it for you on some beach, Cape Cod would have been perfect. For warm waters and clean sand you'll have to come here one of these days. There is a perfect spot for a restaurant on top of a hill overlooking Lake Lanao. I have an idea for a birthday present. I think they send Sports Illustrated overseas, although it's more expensive. It would certainly become the most widely read copy. Send it to the Iligan address, which is about 20 miles away, 40 minutes.

I think politically this literature is safe. The only problem is getting it past the mail clerk. Thanks for the letters, which were warm. *(Letter arrived September 7.)*

Martti Vallila

Letter 8 September 15

Sorry for the gap in letters, which may be a couple of weeks now, but last week I was sick, I think because of the sea, of which I got a heavy dose over the weekend in Iligan. I went swimming and boating with friends, and then for the rest of the week felt very tired, especially in the eyes.

This has introduced me to the afternoon nap, a habit which I am becoming accustomed to. I think of the Spanish siesta.

This morning one of the wealthiest men (Enrique Zobel) in the Philippines flew in by helicopter. I was telling stories in an elementary school at the time and all the kids ran out to see the copter land. He is a mestizo, as are many of the ruling class. He is here to talk with the university president about development. I'll try to get invited to the dinner but that may be difficult. *(It was impossible.)*

Last week a newspaperwoman came down to open an electoral cooperative. A very quick conversationalist with lots of stories, like a breeze of fresh air of fast talk. Heard much about Marcos' private life. Otherwise the weeks have been very much like those before, except that I am now used to things that no longer surprise.

I received the t-shirt, thanks a lot. I am very anxious for word from Marja. I've only gotten one letter. Is she in love?

I bought a guitar for $8 and am occasionally practicing. Turns out my singing voice is just not very sweet, especially when I try to sing a regular song. I do best with improvisation, I think.

This afternoon I walked to the top of the hill that separates us from the valley that leads down to Iligan and the sea. There is much fertile land below, cultivated in small plots, with corn, which is cheaper than rice.

Chris, the British volunteer, and I had a close look at the river which flows to Iligan, and I think have both silently decided that it's too rough to ride inter-tubes as we had hoped, certainly near the top it is. He spotted some horses in the army camp that we may be able to use in exploration.

That river was the place where I had one of my most dramatic, early brushes with death, in the Philippines. One weekend I was walking along the river's shore with the Flynns. It was warm, and I was inspired to take a swim. I had little trouble making it to the opposite shore, about a hundred meters away. The Flynn continued walking in the direction the river was flowing. After a brief rest on the opposite shore, I started back across.

About half way across I saw the river narrow, suddenly felt a surge of current begin to take me swiftly downstream, in the direction of Agusan Falls. In that instant I realized that, by not walking back up river on the bank, I was dangerously close to being overcome by the power of rapidly flowing water, losing control of my direction. Adrenalin kicked in and I stroked madly, without taking a breath, in a direction that I hoped would lead to calm water.

In a furious moment, I found calm. Aware of how close I had come to being swept downstream, on a lazy afternoon, I exited the water breathless, thankful to be alive.

Although the campus has never been troubled, the rest of Lanao del Norte is calming down from recent events, with refugees in Ozamis City returning to evacuated towns. The people still tell of occasional shootings, and some roads are still not travelled, but I think we have to wait for the election in November for trouble to start again.

By then I may be in Manila or on Palawan, the westernmost island for our semester break, which comes in late October. Which reminds me, have you gotten a book for Marja's birthday sent from Japan? How about the film I sent with Shelley?

The $19.64 restaurant bill made me think of the lobster that must have helped you bring the price of my birthday meal to that historic figure. For that amount it's possible to fly to Manila. A dinner here costs 1 peso 50 centavos that, at the latest exchange rate, is equivalent to 20 cents, and sometimes they even give us World Health Food raisins for free.

The economy sounds as if there's trouble. Do most people talk about it, or has it gone unnoticed except by Japan and the rest of the world? I hope it has not put a freeze on the real estate business, although when I left I can't remember that being too hot.

Import-export of some local handicrafts here is certainly a possibility. I will send along some things I would like you to estimate. David Baradas, the anthropologist, knows craftsmen well and they are ready to produce if they can be convinced of a market. Mostly it's weaving traditional patterns that could become dresses. You should get some soon. *(Letter arrived September 29.)*

Letter 9 September 25

It is Saturday morning and my geography of the world class is taking its second test. I am in the office, with windows overlooking a calm lake, waiting for them to turn in their papers. Some faculty are playing golf below, workers are making final touch-ups around our building. The most needed engineering projects here are roads through the mud. Cement paths are slowly appearing, replacing dirt, work accelerated by the approach of ceremonial days, like foundation day, last month.

Yesterday I got the Sports Illustrated that was a wonderful gift. Particularly that issue, because I have been wondering about the Redskins. We get no such news in the papers from Manila. All the people in those photos are so big!

I am busy painting the cottage into which Jay, another volunteer, and a local Maranao student soon shall move. We painted the kitchen red, white, and blue, Philippine colors!

I hope that Hadji, the title of the student, because he has been to Mecca, will teach me some Maranao and local cooking. He was the suggestion of the president, who is keeping an eye on us. I respect President Tamano, his quiet Moslem tone and sincere good will. Some here are more openly self-interested, especially people in high administrative positions.

The past two weeks were dominated by a toe infection that I induced on myself by trying to get rid of a wart with a razor blade on the advice of a friend in the chemistry department, who contributed some acid. I have been visiting the health clinic every morning, watching them clean up the mess and taking antibiotics. I think all is well now. I played in a basketball game last night.

I am certainly not a doctor, neither am I a singer yet. Betty, who has been helping me, says I just need practice, but I have a suspicion that this may have hereditary roots! Like stubbornness!!

If so, my painting does as well, because we are doing quite a job on the cottage. I must share this talent with Marja. The cottage has a back porch that looks out onto the lake, one of the few open views, and I have visions of many evenings there.

If your friend has not yet left for Manila, ask him to bring some of Marja's prints that I can hang on the wall. We have a great deal more space than before, where the one print that I brought along was enough. If she has something tropical, red and green, roll it up and send it along.

I hear that Mancall is looking for a post in Nepal or Mongolia, to teach English, just to get away from Stanford. So it looks as if these Asian postings are gaining a bit of prestige.

I am so glad that Roger and Marja are around you. I think of the dinners you must be having. Have not tried your fried chicken recipe but we are planning a turkey feast for Thanksgiving. There are two turkeys around which we'll reserve and fatten up!

Letter 10 October 11

The last two weeks here have been dominated by typhoons, two of them, both with their centers far to our north, through Luzon. The first killed 40 there. The second is passing now, rattling the shades, the hard rain drumming on the tin roof.

Typhoons change the local climate. The customary progression, big clouds forming on the mountains across the lake, moving in our direction during the day and dropping rain in the late afternoon, has been replaced by greyness, a flat greyness in every direction and wind and rain at all hours.

We are also having a campus crisis, a boycott started by the arrest of some students by security guards. This has given us some extra time to watch the typhoons, to stay out of their way by huddling in the cottage. You should get the August issue of National Geographic that has some great photos of the backcountry here. Around MSU the forest is not as thick. The colors are true. Am hoping to journey into that country soon.

I got a salary increase last week, to 400 pesos a month. Current exchange is about 6 1/2 to the dollar so I am making about $60 which is enough for what I have access to, movie theaters and some restaurants, Chinese in Iligan. It's possible to save for journeys by bus, but nothing to begin a fortune with...

Concerning your last letter, you don't really have to think about the happiness question, because that is the thing you have given to me. The gift of seeing the world as I do, from a foundation of memories that give strength and teach that there are things besides financial profit. I'm just faced with the practical problem of making a living.

I have thought a lot about how reality is shaped by attitude. This is the saving grace. How people involved in the day to day have more to say then those escaping from it on campuses. Scholarship is believable here, whereas it seemed a farce to me in America. It is respected, professors addressed as "sir", signals of a viable tradition, something believed in, which gives substance to people and lives.

Letter 11 October 20, Marja's birthday

Here it is another day chosen by circumstances to mean something special to all of us. Here it is raining, not so unusual a circumstance these days. I got your photos last week so we can now begin talking about them. *A description of photos from Japan, Hong Kong, Taipei and the Philippines takes up most of the letter.*

I'll be off to the Sulu Islands for semester break, November 1. Plan to spend a couple of weeks on the white-sanded isles, as far south as Bungao, across from Borneo.

Next semester they've given me anthropology 1, at last, but proposed three history courses: US, Japan, India, Pakistan and Ceylon. I told the department head that I didn't even know where the last country was, is? Did not get any Sports Illustrated, probably because of the dock strike, although I am hearing unbelievable things about the Redskins.

I have a feeling that you and Marja spent this day together, and that if you ate, there was an empty plate at the table.

Here the leaves are still green, the perpetual spring continues.

Letter 12 October 31

I think it's Halloween. Just woke up from your fried chicken recipe dinner last night, which introduced something Austrian to the tropics. We were out of breadcrumbs so used crackers instead. Made the crust taste like cake.

We have an electric stove. I am used to eating much less here, so a western size meal really plugs things up. The radio carries news of the cutting off of foreign aid. I suppose Americans will keep eating cake without spreading the crumbs around.

Yesterday I gave my first exam, and now have only grades to decide, but that is the most difficult part. Students came to my cottage to explain that their scholarships depend on receiving certain marks. They know that foreigners will bend. I have decided not to flunk anyone. What is failure?

Especially when a diploma is more or less a necessity for entering white-collar life. Some schools have responded by selling diplomas and education is a booming business. So why fail someone, impose a judgment that says no, you cannot pass, you do not meet my standards.

I will not make your life more difficult by saying you have failed, failed at playing a game with foreign rules and languages. I would like to somehow impress the idea that you must do it yourself and that I will help, when I can, and try not to get in the way.

The president of the university recently manhandled a student who supposedly attempted to strangle him. The role of education is seen, I suspect, as an irrelevant inconvenience, to be dealt with in the easiest way. We are all trying to make it in our separate ways.

Problems arise by imposing self-importance. Such egoism is a source of motivation, a promise of sweeter tomorrows to the uninitiated. Resignation, fatalism is how Filipino values are described in my sociology book.

America has lost the art of conversation, which is very much alive here, in Filipino English, a soft language. So I am not going to fail anyone who has made it this far. You get a 3 because you've done worse than those who'll get 2s.

Two girls came to the house to ask what I would be teaching next semester. Was it because they suspect that I will not fail anyone or because I stir them up? They were two of my best students, so I am guessing the positive. I have learned many things about education here. I have learned that what is taught is less important than how it is taught, the rules that surround the process are more important than the specifics.

I am trying to teach students to think in a different way, to think abstractly in my language, in math, physics, or anthropology, the message is the same. A true examination of our education system should examine this, what is being taught, how is it being taught. I think that's what my paper on negativism was about.

My change in ink represents a two-day difference. I intended to send this off before leaving for Bungao, the farthest island to the south, with only a small JAL bag full of necessities.

I set off on this adventure confident that my white skin will protect, insulate, me from politicking that is done here with guns. If I get far enough this time, my appetite for the south may be satisfied long enough to let me go to Manila at Christmas time. But I doubt it. I am planning to phone on Christmas eve, evening, from wherever I happen to be.

I insert here memories of that first trip to the Sulus that I did not include in any letters. My journey began in the earl morning in Iligan, as I boarded a long bus for Zamboanga. Upon boarding, I noticed that all the passengers were crowded into the forward seats, and decided to settle in the back. I understood, once we got going, why seats in the back were left empty.

As we left the paved roads near the city, and got onto the dirt roads, with their deep holes, the rear wheels of the bus bounced up and down. The motion was most violently felt in the rear seats, like on the end of a fulcrum or seesaw. I banged my head on the roof numerous times, before moving further forward. Squealing pigs hung out the windows in nets. Many chickens were present inside. The driver put romantic music on the system that blared all the way to the back. He enjoyed racing and passing other buses, as a way to pass the time.

We were told at the start of our ten-hour trip that, should we run into any difficulties in the countryside (referring to ambush by bandits), wooden window covers, with metal exteriors, could be pulled up from the bottom of the open window openings. The only time I used them was to protect myself from a sudden rainstorm we drove into in the early afternoon. At every stop we were approached by vendors offering food I did not recognize wrapped in leaves. We stopped for lunch near a collection of tin roofed stands. The toilets I saw there were the only ones worse than what I encountered in Siberia years later.

I was exhausted when we pulled into Zamboanga late at night. I found a bed in a hotel where there was too much activity to allow me the sleep I needed. The next morning, I wandered into Tausug villages consisting of houses built over water. Women sold betel nut, a local intoxicant, as well as colorful woven mats.

I booked passage on the inter island vessel that would take me to Jolo. Just off Zamboanga lies the island of Basilan, suspected to be home to al Qaeda affiliated groups (Abu Sayyaf) operating in the southern Philippines, who today make much of their money by kidnapping westerners, and obtaining ransoms.

In 1972 the area was considered somewhat dangerous because of local conflicts, but not for wandering Americans. Many passengers on my boat carried weapons. Some had sub machine guns, and bullet belts around their necks. Christians and Moslems seemed to mix easily on board. The

Moslems put out prayer mats at the appointed times, and, facing Mecca, went about their rituals.

The most striking memory for me of this journey through what has to be one of the world's most exotic island chains, were the flying fish. Schools exited the water in unison, and spread transparent wing-fins that kept them in the air for incredible distances. The water was azure blue. Most of the hundreds of islands we passed were deserted. Our boat docked every couple of hours to the end of piers built from some of the larger, inhabited coral islands, to the deep water. Mail, packages and passengers were exchanged.

We passed fishermen using nets and dynamite, and entire Badjao families living on small boats. It took two days and nights to reach Jolo, "the Texas of the Philippines". Jolo has earned its reputation as a wild outpost for military and commercial reasons. In Jolo's markets one can find smuggled goods from throughout Asia. It is also home to pirates, bandits and rebels.

Hitch hiking, I was picked up by a group of gun toting young men who took me to a beach and showed off their marksmanship on floating coconuts. The geography is idyllic. Endless stretches of white sand.

I would not consider traveling there now. Is it because times have changed, or because I have changed? Quite a bit of both.

I have no idea how close to death I came during that journey. It would have taken just one man, with malicious intent, to turn on me with the swiftness of the current I experienced, suddenly, in Mindanao. With my local status, as an MSU teacher, surveying territory covered by feeder schools affiliated with the university, I felt protected.

One other thing of interest. There is a popular movement here for Philippine statehood, especially among the common folk who associate US statehood with goodies and are sick of the Marcos regime, which is now putting out a heavy dose of anti-communist propaganda in order to get reelected. It may be in the person of Imelda Marcos. Is the

Martti Vallila

statehood idea emerging in the USA? If it hasn't yet, it should soon. The papers here are full of it.

Letter 13 December 12

I suppose it's time for the Christmas letter, to be placed on the plate you have set at the table, with my picture on the side. And I hope there is a Christmas tree, probably smaller than before, somewhere in the house with a small package underneath delivered by some embassy man.

Not being there saves me the embarrassment of being asked to say the Lord's prayer and getting some words wrong. I sure would like the taste of that homemade strudel waiting in the kitchen. Skol! The clicking of champagne glasses. Now momi, I don't want you to cry.

Not a bad job of imagination from someone sitting on a back porch looking at a tropical sunrise two weeks before! Marja, are you reading his out loud?

This is the first Christmas when there are no more children in the Vallila family. That's bad news, I suppose, for your income tax return, but much better news to you as a successful mother force.

As I think about it from here, I think my golly (that's a popular expression here) there is this chunk of time ahead, between a Christmas now and a Christmas that I will spend saying goodbye to my children, as they are promoted out of childhood, by the calendar, a chunk of time to be lived, at the end of which I would like to be able to see what I think you see now.

What will happen in that chunk of time I wonder? I think I have a better idea today than I had last year. I have been reading "A Thousand Days", the book about Kennedy's years, with much interest, seeing it as a life unfolding. I have the suspicion that many of the ideas in that book, many of the words the characters believe in, will be much different in my chunk of time, but that the process will be very much the same, of forces balancing against one another, of people maneuvering for advantage, a world filled with the interest of intrigue.

Here I am slowly loosing the hard crust of principle that was taught me in America to protect me from that world. It is a necessary movement, as for a crab when he has grown larger than his casing. This is not to say there are no principles.

I think there is the organic principle that governs all, and that a large part of our society is forgetting. That is why there is a healthy protest. The organic principle governs here. That is why life is interesting here, and everywhere that people have not lost roots, where the life force breathes.

How to speak of those things? I think it's important not to condemn life for not being what it isn't. But rather to play with it as it is, which for me now means forcing it to be something that it isn't, in my vision, which actually makes it change!

I feel little compulsion to change this place because I feel it is in touch. On the contrary, this is a place from which to learn. America is the place that needs changing, mostly because it's getting in so many places, it needs to look at itself, and wonder exactly what is it that it is doing. Another book I have read recently is "The Enemy" by Felix Greene.

What is needed is a completely new economic notion, one centered on the principle of distribution and stability, a principle that governed the economies of most traditional societies, and sees profit not in numbers, but feels it in human terms. When will the American, so fond of lecturing to the Filipino, realize that the one he is speaking at has more to teach in his patient listening than anything that can be said?

Kennedy got very much caught up in the traditional antagonism, the necessity to prove oneself, and one's nation's strength. What a fantasy. How to escape this trap? It can be done only by those in positions of power, and it will not be something striking, but rather quiet. People will have to try, very hard, to be sane again.

The solution to all of these complicated things in the end is simple, as simple as DEATH, maybe. Maybe that's what we are here for, in life, to play around with all of this energy, distribute it in this way and really to find peace in death. I suppose that's what people have believed for a long time. I suppose that's what Christmas is about.

I wish I could now listen to that French record which Marja brought back to you. Is it playing in the background? I next want to go to a French-speaking place. Do you speak French with Marja now?

Anyway, I hope that I will talk to you on the phone on the same day that this letter is read. One thing I can't do over the phone is eat the delicious food which now must be getting cold waiting for the end of this letter.

So SKOL once more, and be sure that I am with you now, regretting only that I can't physically get my share. But then that's the least part of it anyway, through the body in a day or two!

Love to you on this Christmas and New Year as well!!

Martti Vallila

Letter 14 accompanying a Christmas package

Enclosed are more pictures that should give you an idea of life here. The black and white rolls are taken around Iligan and Marawi at celebrations. Fiesta, in Iligan, on San Miguel day. Yes, San Miguel is the patron saint of Iligan, perhaps that explains the drinking in the marketplace.

The parade was a drama, with San Miguel driving the devils, in the photo, out of heaven. They were chased through the winding streets of town. I would like Marja to print the roll. Those done at the drug store were not done carefully, but by machine with no attention to exposure time. This ruined some of the Japan pictures.

If she does a contact sheet and enlarges only the interesting ones, where the contrast is right, with proper exposure, it will be cheaper and certainly better stuff. I am not yet sensitive enough to light to take proper black and white pictures. Color is much easier. The slides are mostly from the Sulus with some scenes from MSU.

Also in the package are two fabrics: the Moro pants made in Jolo from red Chinese cloth, smuggled from Borneo. Marja, I think they will make good painting pants. I have a pair just like them, so we may be wearing the same pants on the same days. The blue cloth is a malong, traditional wear for both sexes. In order to keep it from bleeding colors you should first soak it in salt water and then iron them.

Both are worn by pulling the extra material to one side, then folding in the front, forming a pleat, then the top is folded down. You may be able to make something else out of the hand woven material. The malongs are all purpose dress. Many sleep in them. There are special ones for royalty and ceremony, red and yellow. I'll try to get some ties, which are a hot export item to Manila and may sell in Georgetown.

Yesterday I took a sauna at the Finnish consulate in Manila.

Letter 15 December 25

Dear girls, I realized while on the phone that it's proper to address the Washington faction of the Vallila clan this way.

Well, the conversation is over, full of half begun statements, the sound of familiar voices. Thoughts in letters, repeated in speech, become fresh. What is this passion for new information? I think it's a custom here to listen to what is already known.

In that half hour, at $12 for 3 minutes, I was there, almost as if I had never gone. But here I am, sitting in the middle of the Martinez house, yelling at the top of my lungs, with the family pretending to go on with ordinary activities.

I had a list of things to ask about prepared, but it vanished with the telephone ring, almost as if I had spoken to you yesterday. In fact I had, sitting in church, and I do on many days, wondering what people who do not have this blessing do to keep sane. It's just that you are not there to respond, although I have a fair idea of what your answer: be careful.

I arrived in Manila by boat from Cebu, where I spent the day with friends. A wonderful Thai girl hosted us, took us to a revolving restaurant. Her name is Nipa, which is what they call the huts with their red roofs here. The Thais I have met, several are students at MSU, are among the most gentle, meticulous people. The boys are excellent soccer players. They pronounce English distinctively, without the power of R's in their speech.

I took the boat. I have decided after my Sulu trip, boats are the best form of transport. Getting there is half the fun. Third class, of course. An open cot on the back deck, the chickens, roosters, in their cardboard boxes, sticking out their heads, and alarming us at sunrise. Much of the trip is spent showing off pigs, to those around, probably also fighting cocks.

And sleeping, of course, with the ocean air, and tiny islands, most not even named, the big ones with an occasional house planted to a cliff wall. In third class there is less effort to cover things. As an American, I have, of course, understood access to the upper deck where I wander to compare. The drinks are the same price.

The boatman thought I was a US Navy man. I played ping pong doubles, with the captain and crew. Ping pong was not chosen accidentally by the Chinese. It is a good metaphor for the East, small, light, played with precision and tact, the spin of the ball is crucial, not raw power.

First class had a Dutch family, the only other white skins on board, as far as I could see. As we approached Manila, the skyscrapers were instantly conspicuous. I was seeing them as someone from the provinces. The water became reddish brown, with a golden sunset, and the big spray of the boat's wake (I imagined surfing on it), made a good post card shot.

I think the fish preferred it the way it was before.

The upper crust watched Manila appear through round windows from the inside of the first class forward cabin, with a singer and one of my ping pong playing partners at the piano.

There was a crowd of wavers waiting. The first class passengers got off first. We of the third class used the plank, to the side. The cocks were making almost as much noise as the women, kids, squeezing into the corridor.

The boat, German, still had its original signs. The Filipinos had not bothered to change them. They had been translated, transcribed, into English on the original. I was one of the only ones to understand "brot" at the service counter. Even the moveable letters of the menu remained, stuck in felt, in German patterns.

Felix told me that his boat was greeted in Manila two weeks ago by the site of a fresh body, shot at the dock. Our arrival was awaited by drivers, looking for passengers to fill their jeepneys. I walked by the trucks, the crates of empty Pepsi bottles, stacked as high as buildings, buildings of thin metal, rusted copper color, people everywhere.

This phrase should begin any description here, except modern enclaves, such as the Hilton lobby. People EVERYWHERE, a constant backdrop, a cast of thousands, emitting an occasional "hi Joe!"

I walked through the harbor slums, my suit slung over my shoulder. Noise, the shrill of motorcycle engines, pedicabs, jeepneys, decorated and converted Army jeeps. I walked through the people, along a road that wound among the shacks put up by squatters. A boy asked me where I was going, offering me help, maybe looking for some deal, but I doubt. I pass women sitting around pulling lice out of each others hair, boys playing basketball on a dusty court, many standing around small sari-sari stores.

I found a gas station with a phone to call David, my anthropology friend, who has offered me the house of his sister, where I now write.

He met me in Quiapo, the center of Manila to everyone but the tourists who move between the airport and the bay, where the embassy, the Hilton, the Savoy are located. Where all the buses and jeepneys seem to go. Plaza Miranda, where the bombing of the liberal party recently took place, is staging singing every night.

I wait for the yellow bus home. Different colors signal different destinations. One amateur after another takes the stage at Plaza Miranda, with guitars, singing American pop tunes. Buses wind in and out of the crowds, looking for passengers, people looking for a proper colored bus, a totally undisciplined scene. Buses often cut people off, forcing them into the middle of the street. The curbs are full of street vendors, displaying candy, fruits, food.

David took me to his sister's. A beautiful Spanish style home where breakfast awaits me every morning, toast, jam, coffee and a surprise, covered by a plate. The piano playing of the two daughters wakes me. The husband is a GE manager. The house is in Quezon City, a new expansion of Manila. The Martinez house stands out on the block, protected by a wall topped with barbed wire.

I have learned my way home, late at night. I have been told not to walk here alone with a full wallet. That is not my problem, a full wallet, my gosh, it may be suspected by those who see my suit. I have spent my time here walking, occasionally guided by David, who one day may be cultural minister of the Philippines, comme Andre Malreaux.

Wandering through the tall buildings, seeing the commercial palaces, the hotels which are of a separate world, nicely done but populated by strangers, talking to the cab drivers, considering their various offers, girls for under 20 pesos, invitations to dark alleys.

Rizal Park dominates the bay side, with colored fountains and a shallow pool that contains, inside, a model of the Philippines. It includes a lot of water in between the islands, for proper scale.

The American embassy faces Manila Bay, where the conquest that brought the US here began. Manila Bay is today filled with big boats. A boulevard is growing around it to match that linking Nice to Cannes. No homes are allowed there, on this road of taxis. The cultural center, Emilda Marcos' idea, juts out, dominating the coastline. The elite Manila yacht club fits snugly close by.

The ambassador says he doesn't travel around much, his face being in the paper every day, to see the nightspots, or the many islands. He made over $300,000 selling his seaside lot.

During this visit to Manila I recall several experiences that I share with the reader here. Christmas time often coincides with the release of a James Bond film. That was true in 1972. I was excited by the opportunity to see it while in Manila and bought a ticket to a theater, unaware of the practice of continuing to sell tickets beyond the number of seats inside.

Once through the movie theaters doors, I could barely squeeze into the viewing area. Finding a seat was out of the question. It was possible, even probable, that those in seats were viewing the film for a second time, as it was as impossible for them to leave, as it was for me to find a seat. My only option was to stand. I had an advantage. I was able to spread my arms and gain support from the shorter Filipinos around me. Not possible to fall in any direction, either. As I exited the theater at the end of the show, I noticed sale of tickets was continuing.

New Years was also the time of bowl games in the US. I had been to the Rose Bowl in 1971 and witnessed Stanford's improbable win over Ohio State. Almost as improbable, given Jim Plunkett's graduation, was Stanford's appearance in a second consecutive Rose Bowl. But where could I see it in Manila? My inquiries pointed to the only option: the local TV station that was receiving football broadcasts for retransmission to US ships in the area.

I approached the building belonging to the station and was informed that their broadcast was focused on the Orange Bowl, to be played after the Rose Bowl, but I was welcome to check with the technicians in the basement to see if they were receiving Rose Bowl transmissions. As luck would have it, they were. I got there just in time to witness Stanford's rather miraculous comeback against Michigan at the end of the third quarter.

It was a rather surreal experience, exiting that station, into morning Manila traffic, and having no one to celebrate this improbable victory with.

I am writing this part of the letter four days later, by the light of an oil lamp. The electricity comes for only several hours a day to Bontoc, the heart of the mountain province, where it is possible to find pine trees and the Ifugao people cultivating world famous rice terraces.

Both trees and people are slowly being changed and will one day disappear. An 18 km 4 1/2 hour walk into the terrace country showed me the long stone lodge, surrounded by elders wearing g-strings, built around a hot spring. My next batch of photos will feature them. It reminded me of New Guinea movies.

Martti Vallila

Nowhere is the transition facing the Philippines clearer than in the Mountain Province. The old men pass the time sitting on their haunches, close to the ground, wearing g-strings and small hats decorated with animal tusks, chewing beetle nut, outside long stone houses. Spears project into the sky, making for spectacular photographs. I doubt many speak English.

Their children, or grandchildren, are studying English using textbooks featuring cartoon drawings of Jack and Jill going up the hill to fetch a pail of water. I was shown these textbooks in villages deep in Bontoc rice growing territory.

Before marriage, boys and girls are free to "discover one another" in stone huts with no windows built for that purpose. I was invited in, by a young woman, and we wrestled playfully. I discovered parts of her, and she explored me with touch, not speaking my tongue. Many houses are decorated with the skulls of animals, caribou, dog, as far as I could tell.

Pigs walk through town. The trail into the hills from Bontoc was marked with caribou mounds (*droppings*). These giant creatures have no trouble crossing terrine that stretched then destroyed my city shoes. I followed my two young guides, in pouring rain, into the hills. I had no choice. Got drenched protected my camera. The rain promised to disappear into clouds and mist filling space among the pines, around the next bend, with luck that never came.

I was unable to see the "cumuna", a rare feast of fertility, conducted every two or four years, that requires a week of preparation, that will not begin until next week. The prospect of witnessing the "cumuna" had inspired my 5-hour hike, on short notice, with almost no preparation. Enough, thank goodness, to bring a rain coat.

The Bontoc Igorot are farmers, head-hunters only five years ago, who today live peacefully around the hot springs of Marian. There are other tribes in the mountains, the Ifugao, the Kalinga, bare chested, who I hope to visit next time, possibly during a dig this summer in the Cagayan Valley.

Soon I shall have an idea of the people here. There is probably no richer anthropological land, source of exotic conversation, background for memorable story telling! This process of discovery is teaching me to listen more patiently, drug my restlessness with coffee. I was talking this evening with the restaurant owner about the customs of the Bontoc, about Jolo.

It just wanders, an old woman's talk, full of information, of memory, which is put aside with impatience by the youth, with bold, uninformed opinions. I suppose, near the end, we all end up sipping coffee, trying to advise others, to remember our own importance, when they are too vigorous to listen.

This process is strong in a land of conversation, oral, like this one, where growing up means entering a conversational circle. Not so in the land of information, available in the library or tape (or world wide web!) with efficiency and progress as justification. There is less need to learn patience there. Raw energy, running free. The electricity just came on!

I suppose this is making me wiser, but I don't know if wisdom is very functional these days. Blunt energy is stronger and will dominate over any reflection. I should write Mancall about my China idea, the prospect of learning that language.

I spoke with an Arabic professor at MSU the other night. He had spent two years in China, teaching Islam, and said that it's wonderful for a visitor, or visiting instructor, but too disciplined to live for natives. Movies are open only during weekends, everyone works six days a week, manually exercises, no matter where they happen to be, twice a day, TOGETHER.

He was followed everywhere, by a guide. Travel was arranged and free. In two years he did not see an argument.

Martti Vallila

He has promised to show me pictures that he will bring from Cairo.

   I am telling all I meet that I am looking for interesting work. Maybe there is more to getting it than talk. Who knows what shall come?

Letter 16 January 25

Last week Hadji learned from the radio that his son had died. He could not be sure. His wife was taking care of him. They had been separated for almost a year because of a problem between his and her parents. We were going to the funeral across the lake, but then Hadji was told it might be dangerous. Her parents might kill him. So he has been wandering around, aimless, this week.

I cannot honestly know how he must feel. It's much like a story, unimaginable. Yet I was not particularly surprised. I have learned to accept things here almost without consideration. How else to tell it? Face the mix of values, of lives. I will always be an outsider here, but I am close enough to get confused in the mix. Last week was hard because of this.

I made a trip to Hadji's village alone, after he had told me that it was impossible for him to travel there. The only way to get there was by banka, the long boats that went from Marawi to all points around the lake that were supposedly connected by road, according to maps in Manila, but for all practical purposes, remained isolated.

Maranao society was organized into clans, it's past recited in "lalung" an oral history spoken at funerals, weddings and other important occasions that traced clans back to founders, which included Muhammad (inserted after the arrival of Islam). Peace was maintained by self-policing. If someone was killed, it was the obligation of members of the victim's clan to murder a member of the killer's clan, in order to right the "balance".

The second victim could be anyone in the offending clan's family. This caused complications, as Maranoa traveling anywhere, or studying in Manila, faced the prospect of revenge from unknown assailants. I was told of instances in which Manila killings were traced back to Mindanao feuds. So much of the killing was within the Maranao society.

There was obvious danger for Christians. If a Maranao child was killed in a road accident (a not unlikely event, given how children roamed in roadside villages), the victim's family was obligated to take a life in revenge. So traveling in Maranao country involved considerable risk.

As I boarded the yellow and red banka for my trip across the lake, I spied my fellow travelers and the two inch wide aluminum covered drain running through the center of our twenty foot craft. All passengers were men, sitting on benches along the walls, facing one another. Many wore malongs. Most were chewing betel nut, and spitting red juice expertly into the drain. (All Maranao homes have a spittoon in a strategic location, and men are expert in finding it.)

My neighbor offered me some, which I accepted, placing it under my tongue as instructed. I soon felt a numbness and collection of saliva that I tried to spit. My first attempt, observed by everyone on board, provided entertainment. Rather than release a projectile, I created a ball of spit at the end of a pendulum that swung back and forth. There was laughter.

Disembarking in Hadji's village I asked for directions to the house of his father. I was welcomed there, and shown around the village. He spoke little English. We were joined by someone who did. The sun set. A full moon dominated the star filled sky. A radio was broadcasting a basketball game from MSU, the only connection of this place with the outside world. I told my companions that I played on the faculty team. They understood.

Pointing to the moon, I explained to my two companions that man has walked on that moon. That America had sent them there. They refused to believe me. It was clear to me how absurd that assertion sounded. How fundamentally different their world was from mine.

My basketball uniform got me into trouble on another visit to a lakefront village. I took a swim wearing it, and after emerging from the lily pads that surrounded much of the lake, took the pants, with my name sewn in red on the back, off, and placed them on a rock, so they would dry while I toured the village in the malong I had brought for just such an occasion.

Returning to the rock, I was shocked to see that the pants were gone! My pants, with MARTTI written on them. I counted these pants among my most prized possessions. I approached some villagers and explained what had happened, in a loud voice, full of anger. They proclaimed innocence.

Maranao society, like much of Asia, is governed by fear of losing "face", of being publicly embarrassed. I was accusing the village of having stolen my pants. I am certain people have been killed by the Maranao for making such public challenges. I said I was not leaving until my pants were returned. Some moments later, they appeared, magically, not on the rock from which they had disappeared, but not far away.

Your letter assumed I'll stay here for two years. I think you are right. I am beginning to see here from the inside, having stopped constant comparison with the outside. There is inertia in the endless passing of quiet days. I understand how Tom, who has been here for three years, just stays on and on.

Which is to say it is hard to make a decision here. Summer plans are not clear. I know of the archeological dig in Luzon. I will write and ask about skin diving in the south, or a journey to Indonesia. The most famous bird watcher in the Philippines, Dr. Rabor, has invited me to his camp at summer's start. He hunts and stuffs rare birds for the Delaware museum.

When you describe the back yard bird scene it makes me think we may be living similar processes. We have frogs and crickets every evening in the paddies just below our porch. I hear them now.

A British couple live next door. Have I told you about them yet? Mark is tall and thin, awkwardly British, while

Ross is big and strong. We play tennis together. They invite me to dinner now and then. Their cat is about to have kittens, which may become ours. She has been wandering between our two cottages all week looking for a soft, dark spot, below our sink, I think.

Yes, this is the colonial life. Something all of us are sensitive to. The Philippines are growing to recognize their domination by outside industry. MSU is probably one of the last enclaves of innocence. I suspect more is realized, but with resignation which looks like fatalism.

President Tamano is about to leave for six months in the States. He'll pass by Washington. I will give him your address and he may call. He probably thinks we are rich. The man has had his trouble his troubles here. As a Moslem his handling of matters with an emphasis on face saving pride insults the Christians, who expect efficiency. They also distrust his security guards, all of who are Maranao.

The students are in the gym assembly hall cheering a basketball game. Watching games is one of the only releases from the day to day. I play for the liberal arts department. Our uniforms have "sining" written across the front, which means liberal arts in Tagalog.

In case you have run across some press reports by a Brit named Gosh Alexander first appearing in the S.F. Chronicle, the report of Mindanao "half in flames" is a sensational fantasy he contrived during a short visit here and a drive through some barrios that had been burned.

Perhaps I should write something similar and get my name on the front page of the Washington Post. With the press full of stories about the "lost tribes of Mindanao", Washington might be interested in some of the ties being produced locally. Baradas, the anthropologist, has been improving their design and introducing them in Manila.

Journal entry describing a Maranao funeral

I am sitting in the corner of a house with three rooms. Woven mats cover the floor. The ceiling is draped with embroidered tapestry, the edges of which fall into the room, cutting the space in four. There is much gold and silver in the tapestry that shines in the light of a single gas lamp.

A man is standing in an opposite corner, next to a microphone. He is wearing a white hat. A scene of a town and square are depicted on a carpet on the opposite wall, behind him, above a bed, holding the body. The tomb is decorated with white cloth and flowers. Squeezed into every corner of this house are people, women in the far half, men in this half, sitting in circles, talking, playing chess.

I played two games (both ties) when I first walked in. The microphone is broadcasting "lalang", the high language spoken by the Hadji, via a speaker in the window to the outside, where more people are milling around.

We have been served outdoors twice so far, first with cakes, pretzel shaped pastry, and coke, then, after washing my right hand in the correct manner, I ate caribou meat in a spicy hot sauce, with yellow rice. Drank water afterwards.

The meal bring guests into circles, is served on plastic plates. Seconds are shoveled out of blue plastic drums, filled with both rice and caribou meat. The young men squeeze their rice with their right hands, the older ones slurp it in.

As I played chess, people gathered around. I heard something about "Americano" in the last man's speech. I took off my shoes when walking onto the mat. Much of the smoke in the room clears out, and fresh air enters, as people leave to take a stroll. Young children are here as well, no younger than about eight. They are quiet.

A speaker has just finished. He was speaking of the man who died seven days ago. Then ender with "Salam walaikum" (God is great) and walked away from the microphone. The idea behind the seven days is to "enjoy", to ease the burden of the departed on everyone.

The naga theme among the Maranao: if a snake bites in a dream, it means marriage in the family. If he passes through the house, it means death in the immediate family. Also a dream of a burning house means death in the immediate family, as does the pulling of a tooth.

Naga osura, day of sacred water. Myth of birds bringing water to the battlefield. The duck just played in the water, so he was crushed. That is why today he is soft. The doves flew over and held the water under their wings to drop. They are birds of peace.

The dog: if you dream about being bitten by a dog, this also foretells marriage. It is forbidden to play with dogs. Any part the dog touches will turn black. The dog must not be eaten.

Letter 17 February 5

I received your photos today, and am looking at my favorite, the New Year's toast, the lobster, candle, familiar tablecloth, the gold frame around your painting, and the American refrigerator peeking from the kitchen. Yes, our house is a mix, and in the center, is the mixer! The mix-master! Yes, it is the little home in this big world, a home I felt suddenly around me when flipping through the pictures.

The weather outside is Filipino winter.

Marja described some of the conversations you had en francais. She told me how she hoped you would begin to put something down. I have always answered the question of whether to put something down with an enthusiasm for the present that makes putting it down irrelevant.

Maybe those of us who really live never have the time, or the inclination, will, to tell others. Knowing well that moments cannot be separated from their individual instances. To make someone read about the moments of others, well is that not really an inhibition of themselves?

My attitude may change, once I see my life in memory rather than future. I agree with Marja. You have so much to offer, that it should somehow be preserved. Being of your blood, I know the difficulty of it, beyond letters to those you love. Those you love are the only ones who really discover what you know.

Today Felix, a friend, and I tried to tame a horse which hadn't been ridden in two years. He was lazy, used to the life of pasture, and was reluctant to take my command. He would turn his head in a side-ways direction, and walk that way, instead of straight ahead. Finally, when he grew tired of my pleadings, I had a stick for effect, and he knew he couldn't throw me off, he just bent both front legs and rolled me off.

On the way home I heard young crying in the bushes and discovered an abandoned, newborn dog. I took it home, introduced it to the maternal instincts of the cat next door who recently delivered two still-borns and was full of unwanted milk. I hope the mix will last. The cottage is now filled with her meowings and the whining of the tiny dog. Ginger, the cat, has carried the puppy from the box we prepared, to the closet where Hadji's clothes make a pile. She seems to like carrying the puppy around. But I they have made the crucial connection.

I hope you wear the malong, as in the photo, down the streets of Georgetown. If a Maranao from the south happens along, he will understand that you are seeking a husband. Be sure to hold out for an appropriate bride-price, which depends on genealogy. Don't know how to rate Czechs according to Maranao tradition. For big weddings, the girl can demand up to P10,000.

Just returning from a long weekend (because of Thursday-Friday national holidays, as we celebrate both Christian and Moslem occasions) in Camiguin ("come again") Island. It is nicknamed "paradise island" by visitors, including American sailors. The girls who return from schools for the summer are "as sweet as the lansones" (a delicious local fruit) and as violent as the volcanoes (there are seven on the island, two still active, last eruption in 1951). I promised to return at fiesta time in early May.

The island is unaltered by tourism. There are no hotels, no movie houses. Four white Irish priests run the missionary machine. I was called "father" wherever I went. The people live a comfortable, if lonely, life, offer beer to strangers, yet feel uncomfortable speaking to any "invaders of their area". Very interesting situation.

I stayed with a family that treated me with a hospitality I have grown accustomed to in traveling here. They gave me a tour of the island, visit to the rich fishing waters around White Island (a small stretch of white sand which changes shape with the tide, nicknamed "alphabet island" for that reason). The sand on the main island is volcanic black. I got some good pictures of fishing methods.

The radio is full of news of Nixon's Beijing trip, the first two days. You are closer to it there, through electronic magic, than we are here in radio land. I heard about an invitation to some MSU faculty for a two-week summer tour of the mainland. I have expressed interest. Who knows? I am, after all, the faculty member teaching the Chinese course.

I don't think it is a mistake to stay here longer. The situation is flexible, I have an attitude which lets me take advantage of it. Some of the VIA volunteers spend most of their time in the cottages. Jay, my housemate, for instance. He is burdened with the unending paperwork of basic English classes. He is leaving after one year. So are two of the volunteers who have been here for over two years, which will leave the British couple, Elton, my basketball teammate, and me.

I think knowledge of Asia will become more and more valuable to an American in any field, particularly business. Another year will not be wasted. The possibilities for summer break grow more interesting each day.

Letter 18 March 10

I suppose you have both returned, black as native Jamaicans, from your visit there. Perhaps the rum in Jamaica is better than the stuff we get here, but probably not by much.

I write this in a Jamaican setting. I am lying back in an antique wooden chair, with long arms, which are for the legs. I can hear the roll of the sea. It has been heavy with storm all day. But I am not sunbathing. It is ten o'clock at night and the beach chair is my bedroom. The room I use when I visit the Lumbocos.

It belongs to a house just by the sea Mr. Lumboco has managed to build by selling insurance. He started out as a schoolteacher. He now mixes those two backgrounds in out talks, which are delivered with a lecturer's fervor, and an insurance man's concern with keeping the other party interested.

He knows a lot about European history and cooks well. Everything I eat here is tasty. From his description, Mrs. Lumboco never enters the kitchen, which is actually a refrigerator and a stove not far from the front door. They are near the front door so they can be evacuated quickly in case "the trouble" ever comes here. It has been as near as 2km down the road, but the refrigerator has not yet been moved. It is probably the most valuable thing in the house (for insurance purposes).

I come here many weekends for the sea. This is the place pictured in the black and white beach party photos included in the Japan shots. There will be another beach party here on the 25th. Sitting in my beach chair, basking in electric light, listening to the sea outside, and feeling the sea. Wind blows through my hair. I just had it cut today in Iligan. I imagine what it might have been like in the land of samba. Am I right?

Weekend trips to Iligan were trips between two very different worlds, linked by a forty-minute bus ride. There was a difference of altitude of 1500 meters that effected the vegetation. The smelly, much desired Darian fruit grew only in a narrow band of territory controlled by the Maranao. Children were known to sit under Darian trees waiting for the precious ripe fruit to fall, so they could catch it before it hit the ground. They would then sell their catch to passengers on buses traveling between Marawi and Iligan.

The two cities also represented different legal systems. Maranao land ownership was handed down, through clans, spanning generations. The government in Manila gave the right to harvest the same land to farmers who arrived and started to plant corn. When the plants matured they were seized by Maranao owners of the land, thankful that someone had made their land productive. This situation obviously led to conflict.

A trip to Iligan often included a visit to an air-conditioned movie house playing a double feature. The trip into a movie theater, costing a few peso, produced even more dramatic change than the transition from Moslem Marawi to Christian Iligan had. Western movies displayed a distant world. I recall seeing "McCabe and Mrs. Miller", set in the American west, as part of a double feature, and then exiting into the dusty streets of Iligan, to eat in the Chinese restaurant that served ice cream for dessert, along with mangoes.

It was at this Chinese restaurant where I ran into Nick, just back from Cebu. He was gushing with enthusiasm about Maya, the woman he had just met, and would marry. Nick and Maya moved eventually to Palo Alto and many of Maya's relatives followed her to California. Three other VIA volunteers married Filipinas. Tom, Nick's housemate, married Beebe, and brought her to California, where she made a lot of money in real estate, and Elton married Rebing, a fellow teacher at MSU, some years after returning to the US and brought her to Oregon, after a romance that continued by mail. I hear their kids are chess champions.

Len, a volunteer stationed in a village outside Davao, married a mountain girl who spoke no English when they met. I was shown a black and white photograph from a visit to her village by Len some years later, where he identified me sitting, unknowingly, in a chair reserved for "the accused" by the natives, which explains why it was available. He and his wife live today in Sacramento, and have a world-class swimmer in the family.

To answer some of your questions, I intended to send slides with Grey, our assistant director who passed quickly through last week, but overslept on the morning he left. They will have to wait for Jerry. When is he coming to Manila?

I should go to Manila anyway, just before summer, so I'd like to do it when I can see him there. But only if he promises to invite me for dinner in one of those posh hotels! We will apparently, and I say apparently because nothing here is certain, and everything to do with money proceeds through next of kin, get our salary of P410 through the summer, but may not get it in advance. I have about P500 now, including March's salary, and will be able to include April's before leaving.

We are also supposed to get a P500 traveling allowance for the summer, but I don't know about that. There have been hints that the university is running out of money. So if China does open up, I can use some of the traveler's checks I brought along. I may get in for two weeks with a group of Filipino students at the end of June, should hear something in the next couple of weeks on that.

I am still using my intellectual credentials. You treat them rather lightly in your letters, but am prepared to teach water skiing! No answer yet from Mancall, although Grey told me Marc said to him: "I understand Martti is teaching Chinese history there!" and then let his big stomach rumble in laughter. He seems reluctant with advice. Probably has to do with professional jealousies towards others in his discipline.

A small technical problem: my visa to the Philippines is single entry, which means that I shouldn't leave and expect to get back. But I hope this can be negotiated in Manila. It should be easiest with backing of a Philippine travel group. Indonesia requires visas and tickets in and out and cash.

There is a "back door" entry, through Borneo, very cheap, but not so official. (Which I ended up taking!)

For the visa I should go to Manila. I plan to spend the first two weeks of summer (school ends about April 15) visiting Dr. Rabor's bird study expedition, and returning to Camiguin, the volcanic island I promised to see again. By then, I should have some idea about China. If I can go in June, maybe I'll go south to the Sulus for a while, then north to Luzon, to visit the anthropological dig, before going to the main land.

I think I should be able to produce something for National Geographic by the end of my time here, in words and pictures. I think they use freelancers *(wrong)*.

Last week a German who is bicycling around the world visited Marawi. He has already been on the road for 2 1/2 years, worked in Thailand for one year. He made me feel restless. I am only 22-23 once!

Next weekend I think I'll go on a journey to the middle of Mindanao, to Wao, with Mr. Madale, the vice president of external affairs, who has offered me space in his jeep. Wao is in the heart of "contested territory", but calm now.

I earned Mr. Madale's friendship and trust on that trip, the first of many we would take together. On subsequent semesters I arranged for my classes to be scheduled for Tuesday, Wednesday, and Thursday, allowing four days for travel, around the weekend, to coincide with his schedule for visiting "feeder high schools" throughout Mindanao. Our companions during these trips would be our driver, a man who apparently did not need sleep, and the sub machine gun he kept next to him in the front passenger seat. I never saw that weapon used.

Wherever we went we were treated as visiting dignitaries. Hosted at meals, given the opportunity to speak at meetings in which we were the main attraction. Mr. Madale spoke of

MSU's mission, and offer of scholarships to Christian students finishing near the top of their class. Most of the questions asked concerned security. Asking Christians to go inland, to the hills around Marawi, was almost as unthinkable to many as a trip to the moon.

He, and I, assured them that the campus was peaceful. We would then listen to music, drink San Miguel, and talk politics with the locals. I would go to sleep, but our driver would continue his drinking far into the night. The next morning he was always ready to go. I got to joking with him about this super human skill.

My representation of the campus as a peaceful place was truthful. There was only one incident during my stay when any students were killed, and they were not Christians, but followers of the Bahai religion, exchange students from Indonesia. They apparently got into some disputes defending a religion the Maranao students considered illegitimate, and lost their lives. The funeral was attended by many students and faculty.

I had not previously heard of the Bahai religion. Years later, when living in Chicago, I had a chance to visit the Bahai Temple in Evanston, celebrating this religion that recognizes all prophets.

Near the end of my stay, when there was considerable tension in the villages of Mindanao (but not at MSU), the vice president of the university called a meeting in the main auditorium to address the situation. He began his speech by referencing rumors that there had been a parade in Marawi, at the front of which someone marched with the head of an MSU student on a stake. He said this rumor was FALSE. The head on the stake was NOT that of a student.

Letter 19 Easter Sunday (mailed in the US)

    Yes, the impossible happened. I met a beautiful heiress who flew me to LA for a wild weekend. Sorry I didn't have time to get in touch with you while in the States, but these rich girls are demanding!

    Actually, the reason for the US stamp and postmark on this letter is that it was, hopefully, mailed in LA by the wife of a couple with whom I stayed this Sunday. She is returning to the States after a five year missionary post here during which her husband has gives up, or taken less seriously, the duties of the pulpit and has begun to devote time to the practical problem of breeding and raising pigs.

    He is the first man of the cloth who has made sense to me in a long time. Half of their house has been converted into a piggery, and gives a funny smell to the church.

    Today I thought of you, your Easter Sunday somewhere near exotic waters, blowing colored eggs, I hope. That custom has yet to reach Mindanao, although I read today in the society pages of the Manila Times that dyed eggs are in vogue.

    I have spent this weekend in and around Cagayan, perhaps the best city in Mindanao, visiting some old friends and making new ones. Some are from the "weather station" in Buko, which I believe is either a missile site or listening facility. 24 Air Force experts are not required to forecast the rain, it comes most afternoons. I can tell you that!

    Good Friday, the day of suffering, is more important than Easter Sunday, the day of resurrection. It was marked with a parade, or procession, through the small town where I stayed. Practically everyone took part, in the winding walk behind the statue of a fallen Jesus. A statue of Mary was carried by the oldest woman. As in Latin America, she is central to Catholicism here. I missed the chocolate rabbit and the egg hunt. On holidays I most remember what it is like to be at home, surrounded by familiar things. You were in my heart.

Summer plans are still not certain. I am waiting for news about China and am thinking more and more of a journey south, to the islands, anthropologically famous areas.

I will take the early morning bus to Iligan, a very bumpy ride, and will hopefully be in Marawi in time to prepare exams for the following week. Two semesters finished, impossible to imagine. I look forward to attending my first college graduation (I was on my way here and missed mine), as a member of the faculty! That will happen on April 22, and marks the beginning of an adventuresome summer.

When does Marja graduate? I wish I could see it. I remember when we left her at Smith so many years ago. Now that we are both through, you should feel very accomplished. Let's celebrate properly somewhere, together, "comme les trois vagabons!"

Journal entry describing a trip to the Sulu Islands

This is a travelogue I begin in Marawi on April 17, where the situation is getting tense. Rudy was asked today about the blue line on his hand, if it was a tattoo, for the Ilagas are known to be tattooed. The boy who sold me black market beer had a marine haircut (skin shaven except for a tuft in the front). Some Maranaos told him last week that anyone with long hair was suspected by the Barracudas of being an Ilaga.

Two p.u. drivers are missing and Illigan has issued an ultimatum to Marawi: return them or all traffic (of food) to Marawi will be suspended. Yesterday I was told in Iligan NOT to take a p.u. up. The Alawi bus is safer. I finally got a ride with Carl Riemer.

Sajid told me today, on the ride from MSU to Marawi that Baracudas and Blackshirts "may be training behind the sacred mountain". Mr. Limbaco told me on Sunday that my Moslem "brothers" had killed a p.u. driver and what could I say to that? So it looks from the last 24 hours that the situation is getting tense.

On Saturday Felix, Abdul and some girls from the darangan dance troop were caught in Iligan after sunset and MSU vice president Boransing came looking for them, very worried. Maria, one of the dancers, is a beauty, as are all of them, really. Perhaps this is a good time to begin the expedition south, to I know not what, but one that may produce some things "to write about".

In Cebu last Friday I met an old man who helped me look for a rubber wheel for my tape recorder. We had a coke. When I told him I taught anthropology he pulled out an old, creased photocopy of a map that he had hidden in a secret compartment of his wallet and told me that his cousin had found the silk original in the helmet of a dead Japanese soldier. He believes the map describes treasure buried in Canayan, in an area behind a school there. The man was there in '65 and saw some Japanese hunting the area with a metal detector. Riemer told me today there is Japanese treasure suspected near the Del Monte plantation in Boukidnon.

I just hitched a ride from MSU with some Christians who stopped in a shop in Marawi and picked up two large cases, both locked. They were very heavy. When I asked what was inside, I was told "armalites". We drove freely through the Philippine Constabulary and marine checkpoints. Our driver knew the guard at the marine one. They told me about "toothpick", a grassroots leader from Iloilo who married a Tiboli from Magindanao county and formed a group to resist the injustices of the Magindanao majority.

His followers, the "Ilagas", have moved to Lanao del Sur and Norte because "toothpick" knew of land disputes there, between Christians and Moslems. The Christians had been sold land and had land titles verified by the Iligan court, but they were molested by Moslems, who claimed the land according to their ancestral rights. Another story about the Ilagas characterizes them as Marcos' "secret police". This is the version believed in the Moslem Sulus.

The trip south began with about as much confusion as possible. I drank rum, ate lumpia, and played charades late into the night with Felix, Minda, Paul and Masa last night, forgetting, for the moment, that I had an 8.50 plane to catch. My things were unpacked, thrown around the house. But I knew we would make it, just as the thousand things I had to finish on Friday somehow got done in a walk through campus during which the right people seemed to appear at just the right time.

I got the address I needed in Palawan, as well as letters to deliver in Jolo. We went to sleep at 1, or that's when the mosquitos began attacks that kept me half awake till sunrise, when I started stuffing everything I would need into a small suitcase, packing in thirty minutes for a month long trip into an area considered by many as among the "wildest" in the world.

The vehicle we ordered didn't arrive, but nobody had a watch so time wasn't pressing us until we walked up the hill to discover it was already 8. Elton went to check about the car at the physical plant and stayed to watch a cock fight. We didn't know that we didn't have a ride (and that our situation called for panic) until 8.20. Paul kicked the ground. Elton came back telling us we could probably wait till tomorrow when Carl and Dr. Rabor suddenly appeared with a car. We hijacked it to Marawi where Paul threw his bag into the first p.u. and started to bargain about the price of the ride to the airport.

The driver could see we were not in a bargaining position. I was willing to pay the 12.50 pesos requested if we got to the airport while our plane was still on the ground. Paul was running from one p.u. to another, yelling that 12.50 was too much. I pulled him in, said I'd pay any extra charge. We had an old driver (Paul noted) but he knew his way around the turns.

I had been down that road a hundred times. As we approached the airport turnoff I kept watching the sky, hoping not to see an airplane. We saw a plane as we rounded a corner, still on the ground, but ready for takeoff. The driver floored the peddle and the rear end swung out on the gravel.

"We've made it!" I shouted to Paul. He was suspecting the worst, that we had been bumped by standbys. We rushed to the girl behind the counter waving tickets, throwing our bags into the check-in slot.

We were half an hour late, she explained, the flight manifest was closed, it was impossible to let anyone else aboard. We "talked up" the local hierarchy, first the station manager who let us through the door, walked onto the airstrip where the steward was about to board, and finally the pilot who couldn't hear because the propellers were already turning.

I decided to just walk onto the plane, knowing the stewardess would not force us off. The pilot has just decided to take the risk of flying with an additional 220 kilos, the stewardess said, welcoming us aboard. There were half a dozen open seats to choose from, available to anyone who could pass, with confidence, the quick test of wills and wits we had been put through at the gate.

The way to pass this test is not with force and anger. Shouting will surely flunk you to the waiting room. A smile and strong look are better, and a joke is the key. Walking up the plank had to happen at the right moment and that first look at the stewardess was like a firm, but gentle, hug.

Our plane did not seem to mind the extra weight. We were soon above Lake Lanao and into the clouds. During the flight the stewardess came back to tell us the captain was happy to have us aboard. It was drizzling when we stopped in Cotobato on our way to Zamboanga. Paul ran into the cafeteria to buy a Pepsi and saw a Moslem woman stuffing brown sugar into plastic bags in the middle of the tiled floor. The situation is peaceful, said a man.

Arriving in Zamboanga we checked first at the Astoria Hotel, looking for the MSU discount, but decided instead on the reliable Bayview, where the desk girl remembered me from the last time.

"A cheap room and expensive service", I joked. Lee, the pirate, was on the stairs. (Whenever I return to a place I invariably run into the same people I saw the last time, as if they are the ones I am destined to know in that spot. Either that, or the rest of the world is standing still while I am running around in it.)

We ate at City Lunch and went afterwards to Rio Hondo, the Moslem village built on the land just beside old Fort Pilar. All of the wooden Samal houses are built on stilts over water or wet, black mud. The main streets are wooden planks laid like railroad tracks (with the distance between boards about as wide). Paths to individual houses from the main "roads" are often single planks, pulled in at night, closing the house off.

I asked about "mats" and we were taken to a house with many spread out on the floor. One, a green and red maze, caught my eye. Walking further on, people began pulling mats out of their houses. I saw one unfinished pattern of blue that I wanted. I bargained down to 15 pesos. We entertained that part of the village for about 30 minutes and then went back to get the other mat for 20 pesos. Paul bought two as well.

On the way back we stopped at Fort Pilar, a square of ten foot thick Spanish built stone walls. A plaque near the wooden door told of successive occupations, by the Spanish, the Moros, the Japanese, Americans, and mentioned Chinese merchant raids, suggesting the history of the southern Philippines. The fort is being renovated and by August (according to plan) will have a stage.

In 1902 the Americans and Filipinos fought here I remarked to the guide, who was explaining how the Japanese had burned the interior when abandoning it. After my comment, he mentioned that the Americans did the same thing, only to refurbish it when they returned as colonial administrators and served thus until independence in 1945.

On Sunday I found myself in the house of "First Sultan Tuha Kalun" surrounded by Yakaan weaving. We reached Basilan Island on the 9 o'clock boat that left Zamboanga at 10, told the people in Isabella, Basilan's main town, that I was interested to see Yakaan weaving and was directed to a trail that led to this house. Many apparently follow it.

Lily, the sultan's daughter, is used to hosting foreign guests. At her suggestion I rented a jeep for P15 and drove the slippery 10 km to the house where an old woman master weaver stays, stopping on the way to see a Yakaan grave marker (reminiscent of Maranao Samal Naga motif). The language sounds like Maranao, without the curl in the back of the throat. Gold teeth and betel nut chewing are evident here as well.

The woman demonstrated the weaving process, which produces a yard of material in three months. Each stitch is individually placed and 30 different geometrical string patterns are combined in patterns set for other weavers in the family by the old woman. The practice is dying out, lacking exports that would perhaps encourage continuation of a trade whose pace has probably been bypassed.

The sultan's family has cornered the market, from the looks of his house. Yakaan weaving, displayed under glass, cover the walls and are the tablecloths. A request brings more samples from storage. *I did not have funds sufficient to purchase anything I saw there, and wonder what has become of the sultan's business, given the fact that Basilan Island has, for years, been the headquarters of the Abu Sayaad terrorist organization responsible for numerous kidnappings in the Zamboanga region.*

A hectic departure: we were late and my camera shade dropped into the water. I jumped in after it, as those in the boat and dock watched. Another diver (wearing goggles) got it- for a peso.

We have arrived in Sitankai, to its long (300 foot) pier and loaded onto a Badgao boat (there are a bunch clustered) for the gondola trip to Sitankai. The sun is setting so I can't get a good picture of the beautiful girl steering this boat. There are chickens near the front, where she is sitting.

Behind, at the bow, a young man poles. White sacks on both sides but we can't sit on them, motions the old man. Two crates of Champion Cigarette (green). The girl is wearing a bracelet of gold coins and gold earrings (like a gypsy), the mother policing the back.

The long extension of the front, carved with Naga patterns, is where the husband stands to pole. It is probably more than half a mile to land, but the water is less than a foot deep. White sand, with long strands of green weed. Paul sees some huge shells he wants to buy. There are many boats in the harbor. I spot one Badgao boat with an open white sail, but most are driven with poles.

The chickens have quieted down. They are not fighting cocks, with their shaved combs. The horizon is red with sunset, on the right, behind the palm trees of land. A few moments ago it was as if a red carpet stretched out to us. Now the color is more purple, and fainter.

Our boat will depart at 11 tonight so I won't have a chance to get pictures of a town known as the "Venice of the Philippines".

The introductory gondola ride into town certainly fits the image. The women (especially) are gypsies, wearing bright colors, gold coins, and big, strong features. There is now a yellow circle around the moon and the water is purple with fading light. As the men pole, the woman scoops water from the boat. There is a hole in the front, through the floorboard that lets her reach the bottom with a green plastic saucer.

That's where the chickens are, so her motion makes them flap. I hear the noise of poling, a boat motor somewhere, the chatter of two young boys, riding bye. Extra poles are mounted along the side. The boat was a family operation with husband, wife, and mother of wife (I think) poling in the back.

Violin music is coming from one of the boats on the horizon...an Indian or Indonesian interpretation of "As the saints go marching in".

The sun is now so far down that the man with a pole in the boat next to us is a silhouette. It's around a mile and a half trip to town. Paul remarks that this looks like a perfect smuggler's retreat. And with signs of development: I see an electric light in the town.

We depart the next day on a larger boat (with a motor) from the "main street" of Sitankai. The husband poled in the front, his wife in the back, until we reached deep water. Then they switched. She is now in the front, poling with her whole body, her bottom pushing against the pole, leading it, as she strains against it. Her husband has just started the engine.

Husband, wife and four children on this boat, that looks like a permanent home. I see a rolled up straw mat on the side which unfurls into a roof, a big water jug, brownish-green, in the front, sunk into a small compartment where the floorboard is missing. I don't see any cooking wares, but I have only the moonlight with which to look, and the boat is crowded with kids. An old man is taking six with him to Jolo.

Now the woman has her leg wrapped around the front of the boat and is guiding us with her pole, as her husband's motor pushes us forward. We are following a course marked by the skeletons of abandoned ships. One large marooned banka marks the spot where our engine must be turned off, for the water has become too shallow. The man and woman begin to pole again. There are well known passages through this one-foot coral sea. We follow a boat in front of us.

The two boys and two girls of this family all have the golden sun streaks in their hair, the mark of a Badgao! Some say that Badgao also have short legs, from lack of use. The manner these boats have been poled suggests otherwise. Perhaps frail legs go with the sail and the motor boat. Mother is now breast-feeding her youngest, lying across her knees, on the back.

Our host in Sitankai explained the nature of the barter trade between here and Borneo: from here, coke, orchids, candies (White Rabbit), sugar cane, white sugar, cement, cooking oil, other soft drinks, Tanguay, San Miguel, Tarzan bubble gum.
From Borneo: rice, pata jun (like sarong), clothes, flour, cigarettes (Champion and Onion), Chinese cotton, Bata shoes (rubber).

A woman just walked in, her face painted completely white by a combination of rice, tree bark, and leaves. We are invited to a Badgao wedding tomorrow and I think they whiten their faces. Most Badgao have gold teeth, as a aign of high class. Top class is sultan. Then salip, datu, rajah, panglina, and ipan, (slave). Today there are no ipans.

I have asked if guns were coming from the south, and have been told no, not even dynamite. But if there is trouble the Moslems of Indonesia and Sabah will join us.

This morning rain has come in grey clouds. This is good news for it brings drinking water, collected in tins and barrels as it runs off corrugated rooftops. The Chinamen in town has a big concrete tank from which he sells water during dry season. Small children are swimming in the canals, knowing they will be able to rinse off in the rain. The family across the street just moved a big red barrel under the place water is flowing.

We will eat freshly caught crabs and fried bananas, along with Borneo rice. Squid is hanging to dry on the front porch. About forty have been opened and are split, giving the house a special, salty smell.

A first step in the wedding we will witness just happened. A long boat, loaded with Badgao poled up the "street", a big red flag at the back. The boat pulled up to a house, some passengers got out to tell the bride that something would happen tonight.

Paul has sent a wire to the air force base: "Am in Sitankai, near Borneo, no way I can make it home on time. Please extend leave."

I see people in the distance collecting life from low tide areas. No caribou here to plow fields. The wedding procession passed bye as we were eating. Thirty to forty people walking in low tide, to the music of drums and bamboo hand clappers resembling castanets, The bride price is carried in a large box.

Imams and datus gathered around a copper kulingtan on which music is played, gossiping. The bride, in white dress and veil, appears, carried by two women. She kneels on a mat, facing the wall next to a decorated chair. Women (her cousins) hide her with batiks and sarongs. I note the mat under her is the most beautiful woven mat I have ever seen.

The groom arrives, with firecrackers. An imam is singing into a microphone. The groom resembles a sheik, with a golden band around a white headdress, purple, plaid sarong, white pants. He sits on a mat far from the bride. (He has been carried in, like the bride.)

Men wearing white caps surround the groom. One, in front, reads an Arabic chant from a book he is holding. The groom clasps right hands with thumb up, with a man to his left, they exchange words. All men open their palms skyward for payer. The chanter is leading a prayer.

The groom stands. The chanter makes a joke. There is laughter. Firecrackers go off. The groom is led towards the hidden bride. Her covers are removed. He bends over her, then walks away. She walks to the chair, expressionless. Sits down. She has a girl at her feet, holding a hand battery that lights her face. The groom joins her, looking straight ahead.

Accompanied by music from the kulingtan and drums, women dancers, two at a time, wearing long nails and flowing robes, stepped into the center of a circle in front of the newlyweds, and danced. Most of the motion in their dance is in their hands, curled back, and feet, short steps which bring them around, the upper body motionless, the faces expressionless. The thumb is wiggled in its joint.

First one dancer stops, then the other walks away. The music stops. The sequence is repeated by several pair of dancers. Then a girl who is very good, the best dancer in the village, (she has danced as far away as Manila) performs alone. Men put pesos in her hair, which are blown off by the breeze and collected.

I am invited into the inner circle by the barrio captain and master of ceremonies, so I see all this at close range. One petromax lamp and an almost full moon provide all the illumination needed. When the dancing stopped and guests began to return to their homes, the bride and groom remained, expressionless, sitting atop the wedding platform.

More than 150 must have been pressed, sitting and standing, on the porch during the dance. Then we went home and were invited next door to the barrio captain's house where Samal and Malay songs were sung into the tape recorder.

We just met the hippies of Sitankai, the sunburns, because they are brown. They're the only ones here who know modern dance. They demonstrate at all the gatherings. They have been around the past day but tonight we found out they live in the hippie commune, ten of them. "Without marijuana, I would be lonely."

***

The small pump boat I am in just reached the calm place where the two currents running between Bongao and Simunaul meet, and just in time. For the sea, in the hands of either current, has height in its waves sufficient to turn this boat over.

We have been rocked to the point where the water reaches the windows. Lilly says that Ida doesn't know how to swim. She is sleeping now and does not realize the fear that is in most of us. I told her to hand onto an empty gasoline can if we do sink, and not to go far from the boat. She might be able to hang onto a partially sunken roof.

There is no radio on board, so help may be slow in coming, by accident. The channel is well travelled, so prospects aren't as bad as it may first seem. (There is a big boat in the horizon, heading this way.) We follow the ribbon of calm sea because it points to the right of Borneo. If we travel in it long enough, we will be able to turn sharply left, and ride the waves around the port side of the island.

We are vulnerable only when we are sideways to the waves, because we begin rocking. If the engine knocks out (we risk running out of gas soon), we will drift with the current to the Celebes. Many Badgao find themselves in the Celebes after a rough sea. The Celebes gets the first RCPI call when there is a boat missing.

The Badgao swept south must sail their way back up current, in calmer seas. If gone a month, relatives begin to suspect the worst.

I first noticed the rough sea when it tilted the roof where I was sitting with two friends listening to their stories, recording them on my tape, of the islands between Jolo and Palawan, which I hope soon to reach. They spoke of the languages, how the languages of Cagayan del Sur resemble the language of the Samal, and Badgao, and Yakaan.

The languages are mutually understandable although new words have appeared on all islands, and the way words are formed has had time to become distinct in each place. All of the islands between Jolo and Brooks's Point are lived-on by Tausug speakers, like the ones who dominate Jolo.

The Tausug are known as the fiercest fighters of the south, the Badgao the most peaceful, passive. The similarity of the Tausug language in the far corners of their zone of influence hints at recent conquests. The Tausug are known as the upper class, with royal blood. It is through their bloodline that the Philippines holds a claim to Sabah, which is in the World Court.

The sultan of Sulu "rented" Sabah to the British for many years, using the money to life comfortably in the north, but the British now claim they have bought more than temporary rights.

As these tales were going into the microphone, the cassette lying on the roof began to slide and we soon found ourselves having to grip wooden molding on the edge of the roof to stay on. Lily came out from underneath to shout us off the deck. The scared look on her face showed me this was no joke.

She yelled for us to get down. The three of us began to tangle in a scramble with others for seats in the front of the boat. I kept a special hold of my camera and recorder putting me at a balancing disadvantage, like eating with mittens. A huge sea snake just swam bye, stripped black and green. A relative of the cobra, but more dangerous, due to a lack of antidote to its venom.

The goods inside the boat were sliding from one side to the other. Everyone inside was huddled against one of the sides, hanging on. It was like this until we reached the calm place where the currents meet, and flatten the surface with their opposition.

We are out of that calm now, having made the left turn, and finding that going with the waves presents challenges, particularly when the two cylinder engine sputters, slows down. I hear it asking for gas.

When a set of big waves grips the boat, the front left dips, almost bringing water over the bow. Then the boat rocks back and to the right, lifting me into the air and filling what was horizon with dark blue. I am standing on the front of this fifty footer, on its small, uncovered front deck, looking back over the chest-high roof. Black smoke is shooting out of the stack sticking out of the roof halfway to the back.

The engine just stopped. We are in calmer water, almost as if the stoppage of the engine announced it. There are 15 of us on board. Three little girls huddled in the middle, trying to sleep on the packages that are grouped there. I thought Ida was asleep. Paul lifted the hat that covered her upper body and found her arms tight in prayer. Lily and another girl about her age (25) sit nearby.

The rest are men, mostly young, scattered around the boat, sitting on the small porch in the back, or up here, on the front deck, leaving the unlucky one in the smoking middle to tend to the sputtering engine. He stands on the boat's bottom, the floorboards are up to his knees, and is wearing the traditional uniform of boat operators here, an old basketball shirt.

***

If only this was a free port. Then people would make their living through trade, a natural profession for Moslems. But this port is closed by customs men. Closed to some cargo and to strange visitors from Malaysia.

Not everything is listed on a boat's manifold. It is the extra cargo that brings the trader profit. Every so often the illegal merchandise is discovered and the guilty boat confiscated. The Philippine side is not too strict on confiscations.

On the Malaysian side they have speedboats hidden in the mangrove, ready to intercept boats that have not been registered, or are not recognized. The Philippine government has a slippery hold, at best, on events here. If it were up to the people here, they would probably choose to unite with Malaysia where salaries are higher, jobs more available, and you can get good rice from Red China.

Letter 20 May 5

Sorry for the long silence. I have spent the last three weeks far from any post office, visiting two bird collecting camps on small islands to the west of Mindanao, Dinogat and Siaragao island where the battle of Leyte was fought. The islands are still full of stories from that time.

Dr. Rabor's "bird collecting" expeditions took me to some of the most remote islands of the country. His troops of sharpshooters penetrated thick forest, collected wild orchids growing on many tree trucks, and spotted rare birds that were impossible for me to see. They shot those birds, brought them back to camp, where they were "processed", their exteriors carefully preserved and packed, their interiors cooked as part of the evening meal.

No matter how remote the village, it was usually possible to find a sari-sari store, usually owned by a Chinese family, selling the necessities of life, including water, collected during times of rainfall, and stored in aluminum tanks.

The animal kingdom exacted revenge on Dr. Rabor years later when his car ran into a deer, causing him serious injury.

And those islands are pretty much as they were then and have been for a long time. Small rice-growing villages, of simple farm life. I want to show you Loreto, where we stayed for the first week. I was traveling with professor Rabor who will soon be there, in early June. I have promised that you will cook him a dinner- of wild birds, I hope.

The people of Loreto took us into their hearts. The family I stayed with cried when we left. I promised to be back in about a year. That would be the best time for your visit, as school will have just ended.

I am in a part of the Philippines most tourists, or most volunteers for that matter, never see. It is one of the things most worth a visit. I suspect it will remind you of Ujezd **(**Rose's village home in the Czech countryside**)**. Professor

Rabor will be full of stories of that place, so I leave them to him.

I share my recollection of a high school graduation here, at which we were honored guests. The graduating students were all a head taller than their proud, rice growing parents. After receiving their diplomas from school officials, each student approached his parents, and drew the back of one of their parents' hands up to their forehead as a sign of respect.

When asked what they intended to do with their lives, they spoke of carriers as airplane pilots, nurses, engineers, far removed from the life they had experienced up to now, in the rice fields! This is a transformational generation for this country in villages like Loreto. These aspirations were real.

The rice I ate there was sweet, sticky and yellow, no resemblance to what is considered rice elsewhere. Hopefully that will not change.

Another memorable moment from that trip was the night I was sleeping on the floor of a nipa hut on stilts. The hut started to sway. I woke up and asked what was happening and was told that we had just experienced an earthquake. They were apparently quite common in the region, causing significant damage to recently built concrete structures, but causing little harm to native homes.

I am writing from Camiguin Island where I have stopped on the way back to MSU, to see this place celebrate its fiestas. I was here in February and promised to return. The fiesta is at the heart of Philippine rural life. Most farmers save all year so they can provide heartily on this one day. The fiesta has been criticized as an institution that prevents economic development. It gives the poor a reason, and chance, to celebrate and drink tuba.

To see it here is to feel its complexity. There is more to it than good will. The simple description one might apply when looking for alternatives for a greedy society. I think the secret is security, a feeling of security that comes from numbers, from having everyone there, following the same rule, not to mention the security of having a good meal in your stomach.

I am staying with the island's newspaperman, son of the man who built much of Mambajao, the big town. He is poor and this has shown me the fiesta properly. I write this by the light of a raw flame, a wick dipped in a liberty milk can filled with kerosene.

When I get back to MSU in about two days I hope to find some letters that might affect plans for the rest of the summer. No word about China yet. I suspect a trip there will take careful planning. The Philippine group had so many applicants that an American was out of the question.

I have the idea of a swing south, to Jolo, where I was in November, and catching a boat to Palawan, the least developed of the Philippine Islands, the one closest to Borneo, with many anthropological treasures. I have been given enough names to pave the way, I think.

Yesterday I climbed Hibok-Hibok volcanoe here, still alive, with the Flynns, the British couple. Steam was coming from holes in the rocks near the top. We were hoping it would not go off. Our climb will be properly reported in the local newspaper by my host. It was the hardest walk-climb of my life. Started innocently enough in the morning, but as we ascended the sun grew hot. There were no trees for cover. The Flynns stopped halfway but I continued to the top, with my young guide. I had an animal thirst at the end, satisfied by the juice of fresh coconuts, cut down from the first trees we got to, expertly opened by machete.

The day before we visited the house of a farmer deep in the hills. The land is owned by some distant rich man, but is being brought to life by the farmer.

As you can probably tell, this letter is hurriedly written. It will take a long time to decipher the handwriting. It is late now. We have finished joking, and are all tired from the day.

Martti Vallila

Journal entry from days in the bird camp

This morning we ran from under the mosquito net at five. Four of us were stretched out on the floor of the farmer's house. The green camp tent stretched outside, covering the workbenches and tables where the birds and mammals from the previous day's hunt were cleaned and stuffed each evening.

The men worked with needle, thread and cotton by the white light of the kerosene lamp.

At five the sky was hardly lit. The sun had not yet turned even the highest clouds red, but professor Rabor's was up, in his pajamas, telling us it was time.

"Now I know how you catch birds around here," I said, "You wake up before them, and trap them in their sleep!"

Already some of the boys were moving around outside, and when I walked to the stream, one had already covered him-self with soap. I jumped into the water that felt much colder than it had last night. (There were many temperature layers, with the warmest near the bottom.)

The coffee brewed in the smoky black kettle, scooped up in canteen cups, sweetened with molasses, diluted with thick cream, was warming everybody by five thirty and at six Carl, and two young boys, and I were ready for the morning hunt.

Rabor gave me his belt, holding his knife and powder shell-firing pistol. Its effective range is up to two meters. I was told to use it in case we ran into a snake hanging from a lower vine.

Otherwise the morning for me would be a walk. Carl had the rifle that he waved in my face every time we crossed a stream, prompting me to ask if it had a safety. One of our young guides held a slingshot, with which he was probably as accurate as Carl with his rifle. He certainly practiced more, as his imagination provided many targets along the way.

We followed the riverbed of large, smooth rocks up into the mountain, the trees branched together above us. We saw the sun only once in a while. For our guides, the forest was alive. Small lizards darted among the pebbles. I would notice them only when they flashed from one hiding place to another, as the boys destroyed one sanctuary after another with their slingshots.

If one of the boys plunged his cupped hand fast enough to trap a lizard he would show him all around, and then let him go. The big lizards and frogs were kept for friends who would eat them. They would point out lizards to me that were invisible to my eyes. I'd look at the ends of their extended fingers, and it would take me many moments to finally make out a protruding head.

Carl shot several birds from a nest built atop a broken tree branch. The blast knocked a mother off her nest, split one of the two eggs inside. We had a first nest specimen for Rabor's collection. (This collection business raises complex moral questions.) How will blowing a mother out of her nest benefit anyone, even science? Museum visitors might enjoy the stuffed product in a DuPont funded exhibition somewhere. I witnessed the collection, how life ended for this mother very quickly one grey afternoon. It's probably no different in the army.

I was struck by how easily the command to fire came, from Rabor, how the command relieved a much heavier burden from the one looking through the site of the rifle. The burden gets lighter as it moves up the chain of command, till it becomes matter of fact.

Each day of the bird hunt started with the cleaning of guns (with young boys watching as they are taken apart). A breakfast of coffee, corn grits and bird meat. There is the stuffing of specimens in the camp while the hunters are out. The hunters return between two and three, when Rabor is in camp, earlier when he is not, to lunch, pulling the newly shot birds from bags carried by the guides.

The specimens are received with much attention, placed on the table at which Rabor sits. When a particularly interesting bird emerges, wrapped in paper, Rabor consults the Philippine bird book to determine if the bird represents a new sub-species. (He says he has found a new rat he wants to name after Marcos.)

Rabor calls out the number of specimens shot so far, adding up the separate days, repeating it many times. Carl usually brings in the biggest catch, 25-36. Didang is next. Then Minat, who looks the fiercest. Didang is the newest hunter, having moved up from skinner, before that a cook (the usual progression for hunters).

Rabor has prepared labels all morning and they are fit to specimens, to their legs, in Latin. The day's catch is lined up on the table, in order of size. Resembling a waiting line for Noah's arch, only limp.

Then there is coffee, singing and washing as the sun begins its colorful descent behind thatched huts. Attention shifts to the cooking place. The cooks have thrown cut vegetables into a fryer, over a fire. This is a time for napping.

Dinner for the hunters is served on the long table on which they cleaned their guns in the morning, and the one that will be used for skinning their catch tonight. Rabor and his guests eat at a small square table nearby. The cooks eat when all others have finished.

Last night cut coconuts with brown sugar was a surprise dessert. The meal, a mix of grits, vegetable soup (chunks of squash, gabi, bamboo shoot and lutia, a tubor), bird meat soaked overnight in soy sauce, fresh fish (sometimes), and banana heart salad. The bird meat includes bats and other mammals, but not rats, boiled with an ear of corn.

Three petromax lanterns now light the camp. After dinner the one hanging over the small table we ate on is brought to the long table where the skinning begins. First a few songs.

The skinners are able to turn a bird inside out, back to front, in a mechanical process that ten years of practice makes look easy. I tried one last night, and it was no joke. I ripped the skin, was disgusted by at the bird smell (during skinning, proper positioning places the bird's anus face ward).

For an experienced skinner, the skin slides smoothly off the bones. The firmness of their finger movements is masked by the ease of their movement. The legs and wings of the inside-out birds are cut at the first joint, their skulls and eye sockets are emptied, and the result is thrown to the cleaners who cover the remains with borax, invert the birds, right side out, tying the bones that are the ends of wings, together.

In the last step, the body, which has been protected from penetration by the careful use of scalpel and fingers, is cut open and searched for the sex part, the testes, if there are two small white balls, or eggs, if there are more. The results of the sex test are put on the label. The bird is then put in a plastic bag for stuffing in the morning, with paper and cotton, and tied to a stick.

One hundred birds, of all sizes, go through this process: inside out, then outside removed, and emptiness back in, in about two hours. And it's time for bed at nine, under mosquito nets that cover the courtyard. We are left to our dreams. Rabor's assistant feared death because of the thousands of birds he had seen shot. Everyone here sleeps well from the hearty exercise of the hunt.

Life in the village near the bird camp follows the rituals of rice growing. Harvested rice is dried on a mat, then thrown into the wind to separate it from the chaff, then fried (till some pops) over an open fire, then placed hot in the middle hole of a three hole stone mortar, where the rice is rhythmically pounded, first by two moving seven foot wooden mallets, thinned in the middle for gripping, like pistons, then joined by a third, and a fourth, who synchronize their movements on the side of the mortar before targeting the rice.

I am invited to participate and discover how tricky this seemingly casual movement is. If the mallet does not strike the very center of the mortar the rice inside sprays out. My clumsy efforts bring laughter all around.

The beat of three or four men, working together, pounding rice is smooth, and creates a backdrop on the days and nights of the April harvest. (The second harvest will be in October.)

I am reminded of the beating of rice in the mountains of Bontoc, at night, in preparation for a feast. There this work was done by women.

This afternoon I was invited to cut some rice from the field, called there by the daughter of the family, who from this day on will be my image of a farmer's daughter, close to the earth, knowing its hardships. She offered me a sack for a pillow at the afternoon nap, and watched from the bank as we swam. She exuded a simple kindness, reflected in the faces of her parents. Her father looks like a fox.

I tasted the fresh rice he brought from the field, the first day a glistening, sticky sample sweetened with milk, today freshly husked red rice. Rice here has as many different flavors as the small bananas I have sampled elsewhere. In each case, what is eaten here has no resemblance to what I taste in America.

A good part of the town just saw us off, with tears. We were close to their hearts. I think I understand what made these islands paradise. Eppe and her mother sat near the beach behind their home. The mother was lost in the towel she had used this morning to hide her tears. The heart is very near the surface here, so near that at first it's difficult to believe.

We have learned so many reasons to doubt. And then the answer appears. So simple. Picnics on Sunday. Hard fieldwork in between. I only had to say that I thought Eppe was pretty during a graduation and the town seemed to know, brought us together on the path along the sea, each of us on our way to separate picnics. She had two rolls of glutinous rice with coconut inside, to give.

The barrio had two mestizo children, left by soldier, one a German, the other, American.

Rabor told me that his friend professor Schmidt, the world's authority on snakes, died at 67 from the bite of a freshly hatched member of the asp family and as a good scientist, produced, before his coma, the most complete record of a man dying of a snake bite. He didn't believe in anti venom. They were injected into him once he lapsed into a coma and could not resist, but it was too late.

The fiesta in Camiguin

Joe Bautista looks like LBJ except at the waist where years of tuba drinking have given him the profile of a ham. And a ham he is, especially in the months of May and June when the barrios of Camiguin hold their fiestas and Joe goes from one to another, dancing, eating, and drinking.

He is a ham on the dance floor where he moves his bulk gently to the rhythm of the hot numbers. When he was 43 and in the movies playing Spanish sea captains and sailors (he is a big mestizo), he discovered Nita, then 22, just back from Guam, and made her the tallest leading lady in the Philippines, and his wife. Today Joe is 61. On the dance floor he serves his younger wife well.

We have been to three dances in the last three evenings and I have not seen Joe sit down. He is either around a microphone or on the dance floor. At these dances he has shared Nita with me. Maybe it's part of the hospitality the family has extended to me, since I kept my promise to return to Camiguin for fiesta time. Maybe it makes Nita feel young. She told me about the American boyfriend she had in Guam.

This morning I woke up late, tired from climbing the volcano yesterday. The masseuse was here at nine and brought me out of sleep slowly, warming my aching legs with alcohol, evaporating it with his slapping.

Joe didn't eat much breakfast. He was saving himself for the fiesta we would soon go to in Yumbing. The Flynns have also been invited, but came at 10 to say they wanted to go to the falls instead. Well OK, said Joe. Why didn't his two kids go with them now, and we'd all join them there after lunch at Yumbing. (Joe likes to squeeze a lot of living into one day, and won't turn down an invitation, even if it is imagined.)

I had the feeling the Flynns wanted to be alone. Ross said that she had brought just enough lunch for two. Well, the two kids went along, and we were off to Yumbing.

As our pedicab approached Yumbing, the road became crowded with people moving from one house to the next. Joe had planned two stops. The first was at a concrete house with a big front room where people sat waiting to be invited to the dining room, just behind a wooden partition. We could hear the eating going on. Several groups moved through, as we sat. We were the last to eat, and the women washing dishes said something Joe considered an insult.

He complained about it on the way to the second house. "Mr. Agham has spent 26 years in the states, so he will know how to treat us right."

I think we got there late, because we were alone at the table. The house was the best in town. Mr. Agham had put knowledge and dollars from the states into its construction. He came down when we were finished eating and exchanged words with me. He said change here was slow. He said the fiesta was celebration that brought no return, unlike in the states, just goodwill. He was trying to introduce improvements, but political bickering blocked his way.

We took a pedi-cab to the base of the falls, started the long hike up, Joe trailing behind. I received a confidential note from Nita:

"My dear Martti,

I really ashamed on my part because you have helped us a lots. I hope you may understand me well. I only hope and pray that someday I'll be with you. Keep my words. I trusted you. I could hardly say my feeling towards you.

Please hide this note secretly on your Wallet, okay? Answer me by note and hand it to me personally and secretly. Don't let somebody know.

Yours, Nita"

Letter 21 May 8

I am back "home" after three weeks of wandering. MSU is a familiar place now. I sent you a note several days ago through Paul Taylor, an air force officer working at the "weather station" which he sent by military mail so you should be able to compare the efficiency of our military and civilian mail systems. I have not yet figured out what goes on at the station but am coming to understand that this part of the world is being contested.

Through Paul, I was introduced to some of the perks of life inside a military compound. The most dramatic was a warm shower. What an invention! At MSU, showering was only possible during a two-hour period in the mornings during which pressure from the water tank was active. Even then, showers were strictly with cold water.

At the "weather station" I experienced the luxury of controlling both the flow and the temperature, with nobs! I can't recall how long I spent in that first shower, but it was surely longer than needed to get clean.

Many of the young Americans at the station had girlfriends living in a house on the coast. The "weather station" was a few miles inland. Visiting them I saw the mix of soldiers and Filipinas that has dominated the relationship since wartime.

News in the Philippines appears to be pointing to more activity. I don't know whether it's just something Marcos is trying to play up, or if he is playing down an honest uprising. What will happen this month in Vietnam this month is by no means irrelevant. There are large numbers, perhaps the majority, of profoundly discontented people. It is a matter of organizing them somehow. Communication is a great problem among 7000 islands divided by over 90 languages and religious "hatred".

Those few who travel and have contact with the military have power. So much for geopolitical analysis. My guess is that you will be hearing more from the Philippines yourself.

In the countryside, particularly the south, it's very safe for Americans. This past three weeks on small islands has shown me the simple, pure life of the barrio people. They react with such honest hospitality to the sensitive, which is not to say they are unaware of the problems.

I got a fascinating interview with a farmer in Camiguin on tape. I will transcribe it and send it along one day because it is an example of opinion in the countryside. He sees Marcos and Nixon as good friends and both of them are good boys. The Chinese who are grabbing all the business are bad, and so is Marcos. People still remember American soldiers from the war. The farmers on the island are waiting for "supplies" from Chinese or Moslem submarines.

I think the US has stumbled into a situation it is only beginning to figure out. A defensive posture is not the answer, although that appears to be the "solution" for many. Fundamental change in policy is needed. People want technological help, something only selfishness will keep from them, and they will get it sooner or later.

My plans from the last letter, a trip south to Jolo and then up through Palawan looks solid now. I think it's more worthwhile to explore the Philippines properly, and see places few go to. I have introductions to people in Palawan and am interested to see a way of life that may not be there long. I think the three weeks in Divogat, Siarogao, and Camiguin were as valuable as three in China would have been.

On Thursday I will go to the wedding of one of the volunteers, Nick Selby, who is marrying a Filipina in Cebu. He was captured by Maya after two years here! And then I will go south. This means I will be away from the Iligan address for about a month. School begins again in late June. I'll send you post cards or letters from my travels, but delivery may be slow, so don't worry about my silence.

I am growing to love Asia, at least the part I see here. The Philippines is an amazing mix of races. Probably the only "pure" Filipinos are found in Marawi and in the Mountain

Provinces, in the sense that their bloods are not mixed with the outside, yet these people are considered fringe races by Filipinos. The Philippines draws blood from just about everywhere. To face honest simple problems can be shocking to an American but it conveys the sense that people are comfortable with themselves.

I spent graduation day in Loreto on Dinogat Island and saw a high school graduation there, even spoke a few words as a guest. Young men and women, much bigger than their weary farmer parents, walked across the stage onto a platform where they were given wreathes of flowers and gifts from friends. The skirts of the young girls were well above their knees, those of their mothers were ankle length. Each child touched his clenched arm to his parents' forehead in a sign of respect.

Two nights ago I attended the fiesta dance at Camiguin where they crowned the barrio queen. Two tiny boys in white shirts and bow ties carried the crown. Some barrio fiestas are being cancelled, near the larger cities, because some fear trouble. I wouldn't be honest if I didn't tell you that tensions are rising in the countryside, as a prelude to the '73 election. But there is no cause for worry. My head is screwed on straight.

Letter 22 May 28

This note is rushed, as all of mine seem, because the person carrying them to send is always just about to leave. This package is sent through Paul, my air force friend and should arrive near your June 2 birthday.

Be sure that I think of you on that day which I will probably spend on a small island between Jolo and Palawan, maybe on the famous Turtle Islands where they bury their eggs on land at night. Hope Marja is around. Half the package is to celebrate her graduation.

I write this in Bongao on Tawi Tawi Island, center of the smuggling trade that feeds the Sulu Islands. All the rice here is from Borneo. It is on one of their "trade ships" that I hope to travel to Sandakan, Borneo and then on to Palawan.

Tawi Tawi Island is dominated by Mt. Apo, which I climbed with young guides. As we walked a narrow trail through thick jungle, we were observed my monkeys, who threw things at us. The monkeys knew to keep their distance. They were occasionally hunted, I was told. But those monkeys seemed to understand we meant them no harm, and amused themselves by taunting us.

I just came back from a Badjao wedding on Sitaskai Island, inhabited by Malay features gypsies, boat people. It is called the Venice of the Philippines, and rightly so. I think this is the most fascinating port in the Sulus and I may be able to teach here in Bongao, at the MSU extension high school for my last semester, if I choose to. It is tempting. I'll wait to see the situation in Marawi when I get back.

Anyway, much love from the South Seas on your birthday.

Package included a Chinese silk fabric bought in Jolo, called the Beijing of the Philippines because products come tax free, through the "back door", a back door I was entering.

Journal entry: the journey to Borneo

It didn't take long for something worthy of a story to happen on this trip. We were five minutes out of Bungao harbor, perhaps 500 yards when I noticed that the sea bottom was getting very white.

I could see big rocks and sure enough, before anyone could do anything about it, We ran aground. The young man at the wheel said he had been adjusting his compass and hadn't noticed.

Here, in the homeport of the crew, within shouting distance of the pier, our trip looked finished. Water was coming into the boat fast enough to almost cover the bags in the bow. A boat following us (at a safe distance of 50 yards) passed, waving. Some on board shrugged their shoulders as they passed us.

Some of us men jumped overboard (I had been looking for an excuse for a swim and was not going to throw a camera cover overboard), and we began to rock the boat, slowly moving her off the coral that her midsection rested on.

There were many black sea urchins on the bottom so pushing in bare feet was tricky. Soon the boat was floating on her own, the engine churned over, we had power. A good way to start my story, I told those around me. The captain brought out king-size Cokes for everyone who had jumped overboard and pushed, someone else produced a plastic bag of stale crackers that were quickly gobbled up on the bow, as we joked about our unlucky start.

The leak in the boat bottom was fixed by stuffing the crack with a piece of cloth. The story could have started in the Sea breeze lounge, just off the main pier, where the captain and I bargained the price of my boat ride. I had heard 50 pesos for a crossing before coming here, and had been told 100 pesos back and forth on the Zamboanga J during the trip from Jolo.

So I figured that 50 would be the price for a ride to Sandakan. 100 pesos, for one way or two said the captain. We drank some more San Miguel. He explained how much gas and oil cost, how the boat had been idle for six months, and how he had just put out 20,000 pesos for the bride price of his son, who'd married a rich Jolo woman. That was instead of the 40 cows and 50 bags of Borneo (Red Chinese) rice that her parents wanted. ("There aren't 40 cows in all the Sulus!")

I kept quiet, then suggested we split the difference. I was traveling on MSU salary, and might get stranded somewhere in the Cuyo Islands if I paid too much more than I had planned. His wife, sitting behind him, wrapped in a sarong, was consulted, and mentioned 90 pesos, which my friend Emanuel advised I take. If the bargaining had taken place after our wreck, I am certain I would have knocked off another 5 pesos.

That is how I found myself one of fifteen, (the limit specified by authorities in Borneo) on a smuggling boat following three others into the sunset. It is the end of the month and many boats are going to Sandakan for pay day. We are in a caravan, except the others are far ahead, having gotten a jump on us at the start.

We have a strong 20hp diesel says Sukharno Muhammad, son of the captain, the one now behind the wheel. He took over after we ran aground. The green and bronze yellow lights on the mast are getting stronger as the sun sets. The moon will be late in rising, so we will have a dark crossing.

Fighting cocks that cost 50-80 pesos in Bongao can fetch 200-250 pesos in Sandakan. Filipe is carrying 24 along, 23 cocks and one hen, (hoping to trade them for a radio and a some 125cc Honda cycles). Their chatter should wake us in the morning.

Raindrops woke me instead. It was dark, the wind was blowing hard. I had been sleeping on the bow, over some ropes and plastic mat that Sukharno had brought out. Getting comfortable was a matter of squirming around, pushing the ropes so they fit the bends of my body. I had managed, resting my head on a pillow whose cover Sukharno had just changed.

The rain caused confusion in the boat. Men piled luggage into the center, out of reach of the rain. Several held a flapping plastic sheet along the left side of the boat, from where the wind was driving the rain. They were shadows to me. I could make out something wrapped around their heads, handkerchiefs.

Sukharno had been telling me of the "anting-anting" he had seen work in Bongao. How there had been a gun fight on the main street ("just like in Texas, in the movies"), between a smuggler and a P.C. They had fired at one another when separated by no more than several meters, yet the bullets had only pierced their clothes. The smuggler's shirt was ruined, but the bullets turned to water as they touched his body, for he had "anting-anting" from the guru.

The P.C. died when one of the smuggler's companions cut him in the back of the neck. Sukharno had seen it all, hidden in a near-bye building.

Sukharno told me another story about an outlaw and his son, who were surrounded by 12 P.C. hidden behind rocks. The son ran out after combing his hair, and was shot dead. The father, not caring whether he died (believing he had "anting-anting") walked from the house, shot 6 P.C. in the leg. He could have killed them all, but took mercy, only injuring 6 before surrendering voluntarily. All the time the P.C. had been firing at him with machine guns. This was taken into consideration by the court, and he was pardoned.

Now it was raining hard and our boat was rocking. I asked if there was a radio and was told "perhaps". Sukharno and the man who had run us aground were focused on a rusty Chinese compass, lighting it every now and then with a flashlight, following a course to the northwest.

Something told me they were not sure. Sukharno asked if I had a map of Borneo. I told him that I had seen one before leaving, and remembered that a northwest course might take us into the open sea above the big island. He turned the boat 25 minutes more to the west.

The operation of our boat began to resemble something I might have put together on short notice. I had given these smugglers too much credit. The storm knocked out the green and orange signal light so we were invisible to passers-bye.

After some time on this blind course, Sukharno spotted a flashing light, a lighthouse! That must mean we had reached the coast of Borneo. That turn to the west had come in time, and put the man who had run us aground back in good favor. It had been his idea as well.

Sukharno rang the bell, signaling a change in engine speed. We slowed down, worried about drifting logs. He thought of anchoring, to wait for sunrise in an hour and a half, at four. We continued, instead, at half speed, from one lighthouse to the next, passing a Malaysian Navy patrol boat on starboard. Their company gave me relief.

I tried to sleep on my feet. Everything else was wet or occupied. It was impossible. I wandered around in the drizzle, finding a cranny of protection from the wind around the front cabin. So we travelled through the night until, just before dawn, we ran aground again, this time in Borneo.

The fighting cocks woke everyone up. There was cursing. Sukharno and the man who had now run us aground twice were on the bow, prowling us loose with the help of long poles. The sun slowly illuminated our predicament. We set a course parallel to the jungle, sure that we had made the crossing. The land of Borneo is not protected by coral if this sampling, chosen randomly by our boat, is typical.

The sky is Cape Cod grey. Borneo is on our left. We will follow the shoreline to Sandakan, although now we are shortcutting across a wide bay. Last night seems almost not to have happened. Except that I can feel not having slept. The cardboard box holding the fighting cocks is so wet that several of them pecked their way out. They are now back inside, under a plastic tarp, probably resting, as are all those who stayed up all night. Sukharno has fashioned a bed, in the back, from a leaning board.

Flying fish surround us. The sea is calm enough to allow them 30-second flights. I just spotted a pair rise together, and take their separate ways in the wind. I have only noticed fish with wings, not the large ones that rise on their tails, as I saw from the Zamboanga J.

Filip just noticed the map on the inside cover of my Sulu studies boom. It extends to the Turtle Islands, showing Sandakan just opposite, and has been adapted as the official map of this boat. The man behind the wheel has the smile of certainty on his face. His eyes and the bow of the Sarah Jay are fixed on a point straight ahead.

***

We are finally approaching Sandakan. The water has been brown for an hour. I can make out six or seven ocean liners docked at the port. The barrio of Sim Sim occupies this side of the bay. It is low level, consisting of tin roofed huts built over water. The second bay, just behind the first, suggests Hong Kong. The big boats are anchored just off shore. I can make out the silhouette of large apartment buildings as they rise above the hills that separate the second bay from the first.

Only coconut trees grow on this side of the harbor, which looks a hundred years older than what we are approaching on the opposite bank. Once we dock, four "businessmen" from our boat will be allowed on shore at one time. A "pass garland" or "walking permit" is available to all.

Sukharno has removed the Philippine flag from our mast which now holds only green and yellow lights. Because I have an international passport I am not included in the four, and can stay the night, while my companions must return to the boat. Sukharno tells me the Malaysians suspect all white people as being CIA, that I probably won't be allowed to take my camera, and that if he walks with me, he might be suspected as well. The manifest for Malaysia, with my name on it, has become effective. The Philippine manifest, in which I am not included, is history. The Sunnis setting behind the mountains that mark the harbor. It has taken us a half day longer than expected, but to me it's a wonder that we made it at all.

We dock near the deserted side of the bay, among the coconut trees, along with other Philippine boats. Huge Japan Line tankers dominate the harbor proper.

We can hear songs from the other boats, identifying them as Filipino. Fish play around our boat. They paint silver shadows below the surface and spread phosphorescent rings when they jump. The Sandakan lights on the opposite shore shine man-made brightness. Here, fish make the light, save for the single lantern hanging in the center of the boat.

Guitar playing, gentle talk of pearly shells. The wooden fire of the kitchen in the back is boiling dinner rice. We all eat, and sleep, soundly.

Next morning starts with the cries of the fighting cocks. Morning light reveals ten other boats, much like ours, anchored in the quiet counter-bay, in "smuggler's cove", surrounding one white and blue Malaysian "Polis" boat, the only boat flying a flag, a light blue field with what looks like a small American flag in the upper corner, but where there should be stars is a moon and sun.

We pull anchor and approach land. At 7.30 we may go to shore. An inspector who looks Chinese comes on board. Wants to see my passport and then searches all bags on board and below deck. In the cabin he finds the Philippine flag, stuffed in a plastic bag. Pulling it out he counts the 24 rays of its sun and laughs.

He seems particularly interested in books and magazines, leafing through each one that he finds. Inspecting my luggage, he parted the Chinese playing cards. All appears in order. He leaves the Sarah Jay and we motor back to our sleeping place.

Six will be allowed on shore at a time. At quarter to eight the race for the pier begins as all ten boats un-anchor and make a beeline for a place just to the left of the big buildings. As might be expected, we do not lead this race. We're next to last now, but at least we won't lose our way. The Polis boat leads the way. It has all of us out-engined.

Passing the Shinyo Maria from Hiroshima loaded with gigantic logs, flying the colors of Malaysia and Japan. The Hong Kong and Shanghai Bank is the plain white and grey building above the pier.

In the immigration office, a picture of the royal couple, decked out in swords, gold, medals. The calendar below reads, from up to down: TM GERSEN, KASTAN, English words, spelled phonetically. All boats are now docked outside. I must wait for the manifest from the patron. Cashed $10 in for 27.5 Malay dollars.

Cars are driven on the British side of the street. I am drinking Anchor Pilsner beer from Kuala No at the Wing Lee restaurant. Most restaurants and banks have Chinese names, Chinese workers. English is barely spoken here and faces appear serious, slanted eyes everywhere.

I just had my first apple in more than eleven months for 40cents outside the public market, ate even the core.

You can count the Europeans here on both hands. They are specialists, like the forest man I met. Five years ago there were over one hundred. Few crimes. An occasional murder. The percentage of solved crimes is high. There is peace, few guns.

The waiter brings me sweet-sour pork and fried rice. The table service is spoon and fork, as in the Philippines, but the food more expensive. Almost $2 for my meal. Beer is $1.40.

Met an American couple full of local gossip: Chinese are not allowed to own land. They own everything in sight, the buildings, that is. The Malays sell the lumber to the Japanese. If Moslem, an immigrant can obtain land owning rights. Not so for even fourth-generation Chinese. Missionaries working in the hills with the up-landers are being harassed by Malays in the bureaucracy. Situation here is the reverse of the Philippines, with Christians in the minority.

Apparently the only ways to get here are by plane or smuggling boat. And a genuine question which is more popular. There's a place here for orphaned orangutans. Everything is closed here from 12 to 2. Almost no American names in the guest book of the Sandakan Forest Museum. Mostly Australians, New Zealanders, and Japanese.

The fast boats are loading crates of Champion cigarettes for Zamboanga. At boat side the cardboard boxes are stripped off (the ones without seals) and the counterfeit labels appear. The two and three engine speedboats will make the crossing four or five hours, in darkness. The loading takes place in full view. Two of the piers seem reserved for illicit cargo transfer from trucks.

Japanese boats that look overloaded are set to return. The man who beached our boat twice says the sailors on board must be considerable risk takers, on such an overloaded boat for the crossing. He tells me of the Japanese in World War Two, how the first took Jolo on Christmas '42, before any declaration of war, by sailing in under a British flag.

Then on Christmas, when the Tausug are accustomed to firing their guns, they landed and the shooting of their attack was not considered out of the ordinary. That gave the Japanese hold of an island that guerrillas and Americans wrestled free three years later. The best guerrilla fighters were the Moslem women who would invite Japanese soldiers into the woods and once they were naked, would pull a knife from between their breasts and slash the Japanese, and give his gun to a guerrilla.

Black Americans never took a Japanese prisoner, he says. A black man killed Yamashita after MacArthur, an old classmate, had captured him. The Japanese would seek out white soldiers wen ready to give up, which was not often. Remembering the story of Mt. Bungao, where a Japanese prisoner was sent up the hill to ask for the surrender of his commander. The answer was that prisoner's head, hurled back.

***

My view of Sandakan changed when I wandered up the wooden plank walk of the Yacht Club. Fong told me that's where the white people were. When I walked in Davis was sitting at the bar. He was very black, with black edges to his jagged white teeth, but talked like a white man. He was from K. L. (Kuala Lumpur) and wanted to back there to his wife.

Sandakan was "an expensive hole" to him. When I asked the bar tender about trips to the Turtle Islands, he told me to come back about one. Now that was not the kind of answer I had been getting around the wharf. It seemed too good.

When I came back with my stuff, after losing two out of three games of darts to Davis, I found the white population of Sandakan sitting on the porch. Big men, big women. Many white shirts. Some British men married to Chinese women, who speak like English women, but without the vocabulary. Davis introduced me to the party going on the boat trip to the Turtle Islands and they all agreed that I could come along.

It took three hours to reach the first island, where Bob showed the man guarding it our permit, entitling us to camp on "the last island of Sabah". The driver of our boat told the soldier that I wanted to go to the Philippine Turtle Islands. His face blanched. "Oh, impossible. There are pirates!"

The driver had hinted at this, but coming from a soldier, gave these words a special ring. They talked about my wish for a long time. The driver was even afraid to go to the last island (next to this one) for fear his boat would be taken during the night by a pirate raid. Martin told me there is something in the papers about pirates almost every week. The boy (he wasn't old) told him there were soldiers on that island. Not until he brought out the commander of the troupe, an older guy who looked like Castro, with the expression of a man who has been on an island for three months. This was the man who would get me to the Philippines if any one would. I made a joke about no women, then asked if there was any way to the "foreign" turtle islands?

"Impossible. No radio communication, no boats, no patrols", but he played with the idea more than the other, who rejected it almost without thought. Finally, I asked him if I could swim there. He said: "you can try".

Reassured by a radio call to the other island that there were army there, the boat driver took us to the last island. The Philippines was three hundred yards away, across a shark-patrolled channel, and I was damned if I wasn't going to get there, on some small canoe, I thought, while watching the unloading of the twenty or so bags brought along for the overnight stay.

I had all my things with me, and was by far the lightest in baggage. I followed the boy who had met our boat to the top of a small hill where tents sheltered the attachment. On the way he showed me the small wire cages where they plant turtle eggs after collecting them at night to record their numbers, and release them safely once they become little turtles.

I could see turtle tracks in the sand, something like what a tank might leave if it were dragging its belly. About the only thing these soldiers have to do is hunt for turtle egg nests with long wires. Usually the eggs are about 33" below the surface, dig them up, count them, replace them, and watch the young ones dig themselves out, and appear, magically, inside the wire cage circles about two months later.

Soldiers are stationed here for one-month shifts. The curator of turtles, who is not a soldier, and lives in a grass shack just next to the egg cages, has been here for six months, with one day a month trips to Sandakan to pick up, and spend I suppose, his salary.

He's staying longer, as there is no one else for the job. (If they made it available to foreign couples, I am sure he would be off the island tomorrow.) On the walk up he starts telling me about that Philippine island. There are seven houses there, he thinks, or so they say, but no one really knows, because they're afraid to go. The Philippine Army won't touch it.

A long black banka is anchored just off shore, the coconut trees very thickly collected, so you can't see inside the island. The place is really a no-man's land, between two countries, where those without countries have been driven. Such pirates once roamed all if these seas. The commander tells me pretty much the same thing. I begin to talk about catching a fishing boat to Taganak, one either called here by radio, (he didn't say it was impossible), or one the driver of our boat could reach.

I walk back down to "our camp" which has grown bigger than the army camp, tarpaulin rolled out, beds, camping tables, lanterns, and food. So much food! The sun is setting purple and I want to take some shots, especially of the driftwood, while the shadows are good.

Martin is very fat, and the most sensitive. A public accountant who has spent ten years in Africa. Public accounting is one of the few jobs in Britain that lets you go anywhere, he explains. He invites me to stay in his place, and is the first to offer food. We didn't sleep much that night, wandering to the beach every half hour or so with lantern, looking for turtles. The closest I got was when Bob saw a shadow climbing from the water, shined his lamp, and the turtle (about 2 1/2 feet long and wide), half body and full neck out of the water, on shore, turned around to return to the sea, interrupted by battery light, in her maternal ritual.

We had a long talk, the commander, the boat driver, the curator of the turtles, and me, about the idea of finding a fishing boat. I kept proposing things. The commander would translate, and the boat driver in fear, or from lack of interest, would say it was impossible, in so many words.

The curator of turtles was most sympathetic. I produced what I thought might be a compromise. "If the driver, in returning to Sundakan, passes in the direction of Taganak, perhaps we will pass a Philippine fishing boat, and then I can transfer to it." The driver barely nodded at the translation, and I knew that we'd head straight back, not stopping for a fishing boat unless it ran into us.

And so it was. During the journey Martin offered his house and said we might go skiing in the afternoon. I began hoping that we would not find a boat, or at least, I stopped thinking about it. Back in the Yacht Club I saw Gary, the Houston oil man who is in charge of the off shore rig, and his wife, with puffed-up white hair and red hot pants (she is bulging out of), behind dark glasses, sitting among the British. Gary was playing someone at darts and wanting very much to win. (He did.) He has a beard and Hawaiian shirt.

It was Sunday afternoon, curry, lunchtime. I was passing the word that I wanted to go skiing. Gary was going for a cruise, with his wife, and others. I noticed the skis in the front of his boat, asked him about them, in a not diplomatic way.

"Well, I used to teach it ...and would be happy to ....give some pointers ..." perhaps not what to say to a man who wanted very much to win at darts.

"Well I hope we can go skiing one day", and took off. The push of his engine was firmer than his offer had been.

I went to Martin's and fell into a deep sleep, on an extra big mattress in his big extra room, with no air conditioning, but with a big fan. The first mattress I've slept on since leaving Marawi. The next morning I went to smuggler's pier, saw four long boats, only to be told they were taking cigarettes to Zamboanga (and couldn't stop in Taganak). Coming off a boat just in from Borneo was Andy, a British skier who was chasing winter around the world, seeing a lot in between, California, Argentina, Sapporo, Japan (for the Olympics) had been his last year and a half and he was on his way to New Zealand, then to Russia, by way of New Guinea.

185

From Bongao he had taken the wrong direction, to Sandakan, instead of to Taiwan, but he didn't know it yet, for lack of a map. (Bongao was "so confusing, he just wanted to get out, didn't really matter in which direction.")

We spent a day showing him where he might go. Martin had a lot of maps. We walked into his office, Andy carrying his backpack. They'll talk about this visit for weeks. Then we went waterskiing and lost a ski near a waterside village. I dropped it, to start slaloming, and we lost track of its location. The much-awaited experience was a shock to my back.

Last night we went to a barbecue party at a swimming pool, and entertained the guests with a demonstration of swimming. Most had come to the event with no thought of touching water. A good number probably could not swim. The all you an eat barbecue was providing a feast I hadn't seen in eleven months. Indians from the Hong Kong boat bought us drinks.

Pretty soon I got to thinking that the party would liven up if some girls were thrown into the pool. An old British man had just coaxed a woman of about the same age to jump in, fully clothed, for 50 Malay dollars. I began looking around for prospects. First choice was the pretty Chinese girl at the bar who seemed to approach me at the barbecue. I wanted to dance with her and then ask if she wouldn't mind being thrown in.

This plan was thwarted when she refused to dance, perhaps because her husband was sitting next to her, or perhaps because she suspected my plot. I revealed it to her, asking for advice on who might want to play along. The young girl she sent me to also refused but agreed with me that a young lady in an orange miniskirt might be interested. There was certainly nothing in her outfit to prevent leg motion in the water.

I approached her, talking with friends, and explained my idea. She wore contact lenses and suggested to an older woman that they both "go change". When she returned in swimming suit and joined the circle of chatterers, with her back to me, I approached, lifted her lite body and with a whoop ran with it to the pool.

We were at a loss for words when we surfaced. I introduced myself once we had both climbed awkwardly back out. Enthusiasm and alcohol had gotten a hold of me. In the local context, I had experienced a "near death experience".

Letter 23 June 2 Sandakan, State of Sabah, Malaysia

Let me begin by describing the setting. I write this sitting on a wooden bench that runs the length of both sides of the SAHRA JAY. I can feel the upper edge of the wooden railing against the middle of my back.

Sukarno, the boat owner's son and half captain of the ship is sitting just in front on a plastic mat, playing Russian poker with a friend. The engineer is pumping water from the bottom of the boat. The pump makes the dominating sound. Clothes hang from just about every conceivable place in this wooden 60-foot boat. The shirts I just washed in the empty gasoline can are among them.

Most of the 15 who came on this boat are now on shore, trading. That is the purpose of the day and a half journey that has taken us to the only foreign country most of them have ever been to. We are anchored along with 9 other Philippine "smuggling boats" outside of the immigration pier in Sandakan, Sabah, Malaysia.

I am here not for trading but just to see the place on my way across the very southern boundary of the Philippines. The sultan of Sabah holds a claim to this land. To the Moslems this is part of the Philippines. Many call it little Hong Kong. It certainly looks it from a distance. Cell block apartment buildings with clothes hanging everywhere. On the streets, which are not nearly as crowded as Hong Kong's, Chinese are everywhere. They own everything. It's hard to get an English speaking newspaper. The only store that used to carry Newsweek stopped because it couldn't sell 20 weekly copies.

An hour north of here by pump boat, are the Turtle Islands of the Philippines, to which I am now trying desperately to get. I could wait here for a week and go to Taganak, the nearest Turtle Island, with the Sarah Jay. I have spent a day and a half in town and am tired of the city bustle. I spent this morning at the market wharf asking about fishing boats going in the direction of the Turtle Islands.

"Very dangerous, sir," is the answer I got from anyone who could understand me.

We are a small community here during the day. Fifteen on each boat, by limit of the Malaysian government. We arrive each morning at 8.30, and at 4 we pull up ropes and motor across the bay to sleep in "smugglers cove".

There are lots of smuggling boats there, dealing in big business: cigarettes. A politician runs the biggest operation which sends two 40,000 peso shipments of "blue seal" cigarettes to Zamboanga every week, al least.

Last night there was a storm and that made sleeping hard for the 14 men and one woman on board. Everyone was soaked, so today the traders went out a little foggy eyed. At least the 24 fighting cocks that one man brought to trade for a motorcycle are gone and won't go berserk at tomorrow's sunrise. By then I hope to be on the Turtle Island, at the mayor's house.

Only six are allowed on shore at a time, on walking passes, except for me. My American passport lets me go anytime. I suppose that makes me the envy of the traders. And that may be the reason we are in Vietnam.

The story of how we got here I will save for when I can tell it, and by then I should also have one of how I got out!

Now it is the next morning and I am sitting in my usual place in Sandakan, the Yo Lin restaurant, drinking coffee and eating with chopsticks. The first day they served me with fork and spoon, but that was when I was new. Whatever they bring arrives on little plates. There is lots of chatter, and the yelling of orders. Not much different from San Francisco's Chinatown, except this restaurant has one floor, is flat, with openings to the outside on two sides, comme en France, not thin and stacked like *(San Francisco's)* Sam Wo's on Washington Street.

The pictures of the royal couple of Sabah are on the wall, next to the clock. They are dressed in medals, swords, and are dark skinned Malaysians. In this restaurant all English spelling is phonetic, of forty there is only one customer who shows any sign of Malay blood. I recognize a table of old men who were here yesterday, all reading the Chinese morning daily from top to bottom.

There was no boat to Takanak in dock this morning, so I may be here a bit longer. I know by now the shops on the street. The best are around the central market, just near the water. It's possible to find apples, pears, and grapes there that I haven't seen in eleven months.

It is now three, perhaps four, days later, and I am leaving tomorrow, for certain, or as close to certain as you can get here.

My view of Sandakan changed after visiting the Yacht Club and meeting the British community there. One offered me his house. It's a small circle, from office to club to pool to houses up on the hill overlooking the bay. Very interesting for a couple of days. And besides, the club had a motorboat, for skiing, so I got my first ride in Asia! My back is still sore from it. Also met a British snow skier who is traveling around the world, north to south, in alternate seasons.

We were in Squaw Valley at the same time, a year and a half ago. He is taking the hippie route, which is interesting to observe. So that extended my Sandakan stay, extended by a shortage of smuggling boats and an introduction to the colonial life. This visit has turned out a little like Manila, arriving there in third class, with the chickens, and eating, sometimes, in first class. The mix is best, either alone gets stale.

Martin, who offered me his house, has a subscription to National Geographic so I thumbed through several copies. Decided that I'll ask the DC office about a job, as a photographer and field man, when I get back. I have enough photos of the Maranao to pull something together. I have pledged myself to the project!

Bannana's Near Death Experiences

Three days ago, on what was June 2 in Washington, I went out to the Sabah Turtle Islands inhabited only by a group of soldiers, to protect them from pirate raids from the Philippines! Saw a few egg laying turtles at night.

I was close enough to swim, through shark-infested waters, to the Philippines. For a moment I thought that could be the story of my return. The driver of our boat, to whom I proposed a stopover there, was also paralyzed by a fear of pirates, or perhaps he was unenthusiastic because no "special price" was offered for such a trip. In the end I decided against any swim and went back to the "mainland".

Sandakan is, by the way, perhaps the biggest logging port in the world. Logs from the interior are brought here for shipment to Japan and the rest of the world. I have secured transport on a logging truck that will take me to the interior of Borneo, from where I will catch a ride to Kudat, on the coast opposite Palawan, my destination back in the Philippines. This letter has been finished in a hurry so that I can mail it with the butterfly stamps I bought with my last Malaysian dollar.

The above is the last communication received by Rose for almost two months. It was perhaps unwise to mention shark infested waters and pirates in the last paragraphs of a letter that she probably reread more than once.

I am quite certain she imagined numerous "near death" scenarios, unintentionally stocked by my casual references to threatening surroundings and circumstances.

I did, in fact, experience numerous "near death" moments during this summer vacation trip, across boarders on a map, but considered part of a single territory by "locals".

I interrupt this narrative of letters to introduce details that I did not include in letters home, beginning with the story of how I got to Sandakan, a story I promised to tell Rose when I saw her, which I did, and a story I have retold many times, to friends and family.

I arrived in Bongao looking for boats that would take me to Sandakan. Word of my search circulated. The fact that I was with MSU established local standing and trust. I was approached by a man who explained that he had a boat that would be going, not captained by himself, but by his son who would be making the crossing for the first time.

Would I be interested in marrying one of his daughters was a question he asked during our negotiations about the price of the journey. I asked the proper question about bride price, and he mentioned some number of goats that I do not recall. I answered that I could only afford what he was asking for the journey.

He assured me that his son was capable. In any case, his boat would be part of a convoy of four or five, so there would be security in numbers. I agreed and appeared in the evening at the dock.

Ours was the last boat to depart, on a calm sea into a setting sun. Soon after exiting the port we ran aground on some coral. A half dozen passengers jumped into the water and began rocking and pushing the boat. During the time it took to dislodge us from the reef, the other boats disappeared. We were on our own.

The accident did cause a leak in the boat, but water was entering slowly, and several men busied themselves with emptying out what was collecting around the caged fighting cocks. The diesel engine restarted without problem.

I was concerned by this turn of events, but had little choice than to take a position near the bow, open a book on the tribes of the Sulus which included a map on its inside cover, and begin reading. As the light faded, drops of rain began to fall.

Those drops were first signs of the storm that approached from the direction we were going. As the rain increased, canvas protection was lowered from positions just below the roof of the cabin to shield the interior of the boat. Crosswinds rendered this protection next to useless.

The protective covering flapped into the boat from both sides.

I was one of about seven who managed to squeeze into the captains cabin, dominated by a steering wheel and compass on the dashboard. Someone next to me opened the book I was holding and noticed the map.

"We have a map!" he shouted, and showed the interior page to the young captain who took it, examined it, and the compass, and adjusted the steering wheel. The rough sea made reading a precise direction from the compass impossible, in my opinion, but I was happy to contribute my map to the effort.

I did not sleep that night. Nor did any of my boat mates, as far as I could tell. The noise of the engine, the storm, the fighting cocks kept us on alert. I was thinking that if we sank, I would vanish from this earth without leaving any trace.

The storm ceased. Our engine, thankfully, did not. Sunrise brought calm water and fog. Our captain, using my map, steered us in a direction that eventually brought us near land. We ran aground a second time, this time, gratefully. There was nothing but jungle visible. We turned to the right, or north, and followed the coastline until we saw seaside villages and ultimately Sandakan.

The trip to Sandakan was not my closest brush with death on that boat. After a week of unsuccessful efforts to find transit to the Philippine Turtle Islands, for reasons explained in my letter, I boarded the Shara Jay for their trip back to Sandakan, insisting that they detour to the Turtle Islands and drop me off.

The captain refused, referring again to the pirates that were known to use the islands to hide. I was insistent. I did not want to return to Bungao. We had a standoff. At that moment is would have been easy for one or more of the passengers to solve their problem by cutting off my head, and throwing me overboard, I realize in retrospect. Instead, the captain turned the boat around, dropped me off in Sandakan, wishing me good luck.

That afternoon I negotiated the logging truck trip to the interior. I spent that night among Chinese loggers who I felt were deeply suspicious of me. They explained that we were in one of the few regions of the world still inhabited by wild orangutans. They were harvesting massive trees, driving the orangutans deeper into the forest. The demand of bowling alley construction in Japan was destroying the countryside.

The next morning I rode by jeep to Kota Kinabalu, capital of the state of Sabah, where I spent the night on a cot in a hotel lobby. I found a ride to Kudat where it took me a couple of days to locate a rice boat heading for Palawan. That boat was so full of rice bags that it could not have possibly survived a storm like the one the Sarah Jay experienced. The water was inches from our heavily laden.

This captain was experienced. The sea remained calm. I spent the precarious overnight passage sleeping among the rice bags. We reached jungle land around the middle of the next day. The captain explained that I could take a small boat that came out to greet us back to the island, as we would have to await sunset to travel further. I took him up on the invitation and was welcomed into a small nipa hut barely visible from the sea.

As sunset approached, we proceeded further north on Balabac Island. It was pitch black when we reached the mouth of a river where our boat was met by men carrying burning palm leaves that lit our route upriver, inland. There was talk in languages I did not understand. I was invited to a house where there were many men. When I explained that I had come from the Sulus, there was excitement, and much interest about any details I could provide about the "situation" there.

I told them about my MSU teaching job, shared observations that I was not inventing, realizing that there was not much of substance I could contribute. I sensed an insurgency against the central government, a distant entity to everyone in the south, a region operating with its own rules, its own religion. They offered me a place to sleep till sunrise.

The next morning I returned to the boat, now empty. The rice had been unloaded while I slept. The last traces of rice were swept into the water by the captain just before we arrived in the port of Balabac, where we were carefully inspected by officials. I was feeling a discomfort in my ear that I suspected may have been caused by an insect from one of the rice bags that had served as a pillow.

On Balabac, known as "bird island", I was invited into the home of an American who had lived there for many years. We talked in general. I got the sense that he was on this remote island for reasons he was not ready to share with a stranger. The pain in my ear was increasing. I am sure I slept that night, but remember being kept awake by the pain.

I got a ride on a swift police boat the next day to nearby Palawan, to Brooks Pointe. My goal was Puerto Princesa where I had the address of an MSU student. A truck ride got me there by sunset.

The countryside I passed through on the way was reminiscent of what I had seen on many drives along the coast of Mindanao. A dirt road, palm trees leaning into the sea on one side, a scattering of nipa huts on the interior side of the road, families with many children sitting around, and under, houses on stilts, dogs, goats, chickens not paying much attention to passing traffic.

Wrecks of jeeps could be seen in some yards. Bicycles, some with small engines, appeared to be the preferred method of transport.

Getting rides was not a problem for me. English is spoken everywhere, a wandering American is approached by village kids, and reasonable requests are accommodated by the human web that ties society together. As an MSU teacher I had local status. I had been in the Philippines long enough that I was speaking English in the Filipino manner, accentuating the end of sentences.

It is difficult for someone who has not lived the experience to appreciate the sincere open heartedness of the island people. When I arrived at the address I had in Puerto Princesa, I was welcomed as a family member, shown a room where I could sleep, introduced to members of the extended family, and given the name of a local doctor who had a look at my ear.

There was serious swelling. He gave me some pain killing tablets, which I took immediately. That night something burst, relieving the pain. My hearing was fine. The next morning I heard a clear voice repeat "good morning" several times. I looked into the adjacent room from where the sound was coming and saw a black bird, with a yellow collar.

The bird repeated "good morning" to me in person. My host explained it was a Tiao bird. If a Tiao bird is raised alone, in its cage, it mimics the language spoken to it. If Tiao birds are put in a cage together, they do not learn human words. They are also sensitive to surrounding emotions, known to die if their owner expresses or experiences shock.

I spent a couple of days in Puerto Princesa exploring the town and lining up transport on a fishing vessel that took me to Iloilo. That journey took two days during which I observed the use of large nets, and circular maneuvers, to capture large quantities of fish.

Once back "in civilization", it was no problem getting to Manila. Just about everyone I connected with was glad to see me, and told me to contact my mother! IMMEDIATLY! Rose had apparently cast a net of her own on the Islands.

Having filled the reader in on what happened in the interlude, I now return to the collection of letters.

Letter 24 July 7 arrived September 2nd! *after a silence of two months....*

Came back this morning to MSU find several letters. Most of them were from you. Was in Manila to meet four new volunteers and am feeling very much a part of VIA now. I remembered arriving last year, and now I was greeting new volunteers, taking them to some of the restaurants I have discovered in Manila. I am growing familiar with the city, particularly the buses.

David Baradas, the anthropologist, is living there now and about to be named research director for the Panamin Foundation, the Elizalde funded group that "discovered" the Tasaday, the "lost tribe". The Tasaday are known everywhere now. Panamin is rumored to be looking for gold, and other minerals, in those hills, so the project is not without commercial interest.

I am growing familiar with the subject matter here and am taking fewer slides, being more selective. Met a Belgian TV man in Manila who may come to Mindanao to film. I also sat in on a meeting of the SE Asian Archeologist and learned of a dig and archeological training project next summer in the caves of Palawan. I passed through Palawan on my way back from Sabah, first to Balabac, the island of talking birds. I got there on a small boat from Kudat, on the western coast of Sabah, that was smuggling rice. I got to Brooks Point on a patrol boat hunting smugglers, so I saw the smuggling operation from both sides. This makes me an expert on the economy of the south, most of which is illegal.

The Chinese silk bought in Jolo is one example. Government officials get money from bribing smugglers, and the smugglers make money circumventing rules and taxes so the relationship is symbiotic, and casual in a way possible only in the Philippines.

I noticed a sharp contrast between the serious Chinese in Sandakan and the casual Filipinos. From Brooks Point I rode a truck to Puerto Princesa, the capital of Palawan. My stay there was dominated by an earache I must have gotten from some animal who rode with me on the rice bags.

This gave me a chance to meet doctors in Palawan who have their hands full fighting malaria, a strain there can kill in 18 hours. The antibiotics took effect by the time I reached Cuyo Island, home of some of the loveliest MSU students, one has just been named Miss Labor of the Philippines.

I then spent a night on a fishing boat in the richest fishing grounds of the Philippines before riding to Iloilo on a boat carrying the fish to market. From there I found a plane to Cagayan de Oro and was, with what seemed like magic, suddenly back to the place I had left two months ago.

Classes have started, although for the above reasons mine are not yet organized. I have found books, so it should be easier than last year, courses in Chinese history, geography of the world, of which I experience more each vacation, and economic anthropology. More soon.

Letter 25 August 1

Yesterday I found your telegram in the post office. It lay there for a week, because no one has gone down to Iligan to pick mail up since last weekend. By now I hope you have gotten one of the notes I have sent so I don't think there is a need to wire. My long silence was due to passage through Balabac and Palawan, parts of the Philippines that don't specialize in mail service!

Then, when I got back to MSU, a few days late, I left immediately for Manila to greet the new volunteers. The rush there was so hectic, the rains were just beginning and the traffic was as snarled as the bureaucracy. I've experienced the latter before, but the torrential rain was special. Before I could think, I was on the 3am discount flight south with the new volunteers, without mailing a note begun long before.

Life here began, after the three-month flurry, to resemble the day-to-day, understanding that there really are no such things as "ordinary days" in Mindanao. That, according to a foreign professor, is one of its main attractions.

The semester started with a faculty strike, or the threat of one, which produced a "dialogue" between the faculty and the administration. The main issue was security. The houses of several faculty members have been robbed. They were the moving force behind demands that included better faucets, with running water, for the boys dormitory, more lighting on campus.

A gun is part of the not-so-traditional Maranao costume, and although there have not been many incidents, the loose firearms do frighten some people, mostly the Christians.

The dialogue resulted in sweet promises which, when put to an objective test, didn't have much substance. Security remains a problem, and the poverty of many does much to explain it. Food prices have more than doubled since the last election, with no extra money coming in. Over the summer the situation in Marawi was tense. Caused by a blockade by Iligan merchants who refused to drive anything up the hill.

This skyrocketed the prices and forced many below the subsistence level. Some of the hajis who peddle who peddle artifacts have been agreeing to very low prices for their handicrafts, a sure sign that times are hard. This ordinarily happens around Ramadan, the month of fasting, when Moslems have large evening meals after sunset.

The beginning of school brought relief, I hoped, judging from the planting of corn on both sides of the road between here and Iligan. During tense times no one cultivates this middle ground between the Christian coast and Moslem interior.

President Tamano has just returned from a five-month tour of the US and Egypt, where he may soon be ambassador, many think, and this afternoon he reported on his trip. He spoke of the many demonstrations they were having in the States. I was named to a reception committee to plan a welcome home dinner, but in keeping with efficiency lessons that Tamano must have learned in the States, he decided to cancel the dinner as being too extravagant.

During the past two weekends I have gone to Nawan, a small quiet Christian town where Paul, a new volunteer, is being hosted by the mayor. A storm was threatening and the waves were good for body surfing. While Luzon has recently been swamped, Mindanao remains dry during what is supposed to be the wet season.

(Paul turned out to be an adventurer, willing to join me on weekend trips to numerous destinations. I was happy to introduce him to friends in Camiguin Island, and to discover new places. We got into the habit of riding on the roofs of buses, instead of being crammed inside.

One trip we made together was an expedition inland, along a river not far from Nawan, to collect and study bats.

We drove along the river in jeeps in darkness, using only flashlights, so as not to disturb our targets of study. The bats were caught in nets spread across the narrow river. They were carefully dislodged from the nets, catalogued, and then consumed, tasting like chicken.

One economic project his host mayor was championing was the development of fish farms, representing a diversification of the local economy. Too much of the Philippines was suffering from the harvesting of natural resources, with no attention paid to replenishment. This was most dramatically seen during bus rides through countryside denuded of tropical forest. When rains came to such unprotected land, precious topsoil was washed into the sea.)

We were barely able to escape Manila because of the rain, which has not stopped. Next weekend we are planning a trip to local mountains with waterfalls, but we are worried because the rivers here are running so low. We will try, and camp at one of Dr. Rabor's sites where he collects bats.

Each day the papers here report more damage in the north. A lake flooded yesterday, swamping 16 towns. A rumor is circulating Manila that Marcos wants the election delayed for two years because they shouldn't be held so soon after a disaster. This is only his latest attempt, if true.

A shipload of arms was discovered off the Luzon coast, and many believe it's the beginning of a Marcos attempt to create a situation forcing martial law by election time. Even weather gets into politics here!

The rice terraces of the mountain province I visited at Christmas time are flooded. Most of Manila's vegetables are grown there. Much of inland Luzon is a lake, judging from news photos. All this at a time the economy is unsteady. A good part of any relief aid will undoubtedly go into the pockets of a few people. That, in brief, is the national scene.

Down here in Mindanao we are isolated from some of the intrigue of the political system up north, and we seem to be spared its weather as well. Our problems are of a different nature.

The Flynns, the British couple next door, are flying to England for Christmas. They've been here two years, and are due a flight before returning for a third year. When I think about that flight I realize that it is impossible for me to consider that this place and London, Rehoboth, or Washington exist on the same world, at the same time. In many African societies, initiation rites into adulthood for a man consist of being taken into the woods, or a distant village, for periods as long as two years. I think the idea is to show how fragile, relative, human organization is. I am learning some of that here.

Letter 26 August 10

Last week I was told there was a letter waiting for me in President Tamano's office. An invitation to a "pagana Maranao", perhaps, I thought. We have not had a celebration since Tamano left for his five-month tour of the States. He is now back, and celebrations would begin again!

Or maybe he wanted to tell me about his trip to my country. I found the note in my office after lunch. It was more then a note, included clippings attached, one from the consul in Cebu, a man named Sullivan who I met last year during his visit to MSU, asking where I have last been seen, where was I going, where could I be found? Cable back urgently because mother suspects he is in a cooking pot somewhere!

I was flattered by how quickly the vast American communication networks had been mobilized. Even with America's electronic power it would have been very hard to find me out there somewhere in Palawan with malaria carrying mosquitoes laying their eggs in my eyes.

I was back on campus, returning, slowly, to the day-to-day, but now with several telegrams to send.

Everyone around the president's office has been informed and was worried. I heard jokes about it for weeks. Sending telegrams to the US is no joke on a salary of P410 a month, at $30 for 22 words. And another to Sullivan in Cebu.

An imagination that had worked itself into a fabricated frenzy on the other side of the globe was calmed. Here, the mood changed very little. Ah, subjectivity! I won't say that I wasn't pleased by the worry, but that I would probably have been more so without it...and bringing Fulbright into it!

I got your August 2nd letter today, telling me your side of the drama. Sounds more exciting than my journey! For future reference, the fastest way to get in touch is by telegram direct to MSU. We hear from the mailbox in Iligan about once a week, so a telegram can sit there, stirring imaginations for too long.

It is raining hard. This is unusual, and welcome. The first hard rain in more than a month. The Flynns and I have been invited to the Flores for dinner and bridge. I have been getting up early to play tennis with Ross on a dry court at 6.30. Tomorrow I can sleep late.

It is now the afternoon of the next day. The rain has not stopped. The roof is loud for the first time in months and everyone is huddled somewhere indoors. I am thinking of the 10-minute walk I face, on the muddy sloping hill from our cottage, across the third and fourth holes of the golf course, and on to the social science building, where I have promised to return exams to my 4 o'clock geography class. Doubt many students will show up.

The walk will not be in vain. MSU shows very different colors during a rain. Everything is green. The caribou jump around like bronco bulls. Dark clouds hang above the lake. I wish for a fireplace.

Mark Flynn and I had very bad cards last night (a good sign for the heart, I hope) and we played them not so well. But the dinner was good.

This weekend I will fly to Jolo, in the Sulus, for an anthropological conference on the Tausug, the "boat people", a good way to meet experts in the field. Am using money I have saved up. Then next week the MSU faculty basketball team returns to Domaguete City, to play Sillivan University, and once again celebrate my birthday in the "home of gentle people".

Letter 27 August 31

Many thanks for the letters I have begun to receive regularly, especially the last one, dated August 19 which arrived yesterday with news of next summer's proposed trip. My first reaction is that the semester here ends in late April so that would be the best time to arrive in Marawi, to witness graduation, which will be my first here, as I was away last year.

Check with the Rabors. I think he has a plan to return next summer with DuPont money and collect birds on some of the smaller islands. If so, we have a standing invitation. In Jolo two weeks ago I met the anthropology crowd from Manila and there would be no problem with me joining. This will become clearer by Christmas.

As for the National Geographic article, I will prepare a piece on the rice planting ritual I witnessed and photographed here last year, important because it shows the undercurrent of pre-Islamic practices that are still very much alive among these Moslems. Four of us plan to present a short paper on this in Cagayan de Oro in November, using my slides, so that will give me a chance to formalize the material.

Maybe Marja could make a trip here. It certainly is artistically stimulating. I know of at least half a dozen novelists who are living out the rest of their days on the tiny islands south of Palawan, and a lot of painters have had tropical stimulation.

Some former volunteers now stay in Cebu. Nick got married last year and now lives there.

There is a direct flight from Davao to Indonesia and Bali, so it is no longer necessary to exit from Manila. So it seems the best program after the Philippines would be a southern exit, flight from Mindanao to Bali, then a boat to Djakarta. The Philippines can be very inexpensive, and there is enough to see to fill 3-4 weeks.

The weeks continue to be interrupted by messages asking about my whereabouts. Last week it was Sulse who had heard from Zobel, the rich man who flew here by helicopter last year. He is honorary Sultan of Marawi and probably has more connections with Moslems than anyone else in Manila and has big plans for the development of SE Asia.

Letter 28 September 23

Hugh Gibb, a well-known British documentary filmmaker has been at MSU for the past four days, documenting the Maranao and I have been following him to events he always seems to find, creating most of them with the presence of his camera.

We wandered into a burial yesterday. The pace has been so hectic that this morning's news, of the burial of constitutional rights in the Philippines, came as just another current event, movie-like. That picture is not being directed by a small group in search of aesthetic pleasure.

It is Saturday and reaction to Marcos' declaration of martial law is subdued, but students are meeting to decide on a response. Some want to go home, fearing that by Monday the army will be here and that many will be held accountable for their political views. The radio this morning told of the arrest of some students in Manila. No paper today.

For weeks there has been speculation on when this would happen. The papers told of bombings each day in Manila, events orchestrated to reach some climax. Last week a bomb went off in the bathroom of the hall where the constitutional convention meets. Late last night defense secretary Enrile's jeep was ambushed. He was not in it. Marcos declared martial law hours later.

Hugh Gibb arrived five days ago and since then has demonstrated to me to power of the director. I gave a slide show on Thursday night to several hundred students in the science-building hall. The night before the show, John, one of Mr. Gibb's assistants, and I arranged my slides in a sequence that would suggest a story.

John was having an easier time, for he was unrestricted by the memory of shots in their true sequence, and was thus free to build a story of his choosing. As I explained the slides the next night, I could see that the impressions left on students' minds had little to do with how I had experienced the shots, and everything to do with the direction, how they were organized.

Anyone in the audience armed with a map of the Philippines would easily have discovered the trickery of my storytelling. I was defying the laws of geography in my sequence (the show was officially hosted by my geography of the world class). To see my slides, all were sitting in the dark.

I showed photos of the rice planting ritual across the lake, then shots from Wao, on the other side of the high mountains which form the silhouette of the sleeping lady, then photos from last year's trip to the mountain province, to which I am returning this semester break. Everyone seemed to enjoy the show.

Mr. Gibb suggested there is a market for such productions, and I have been inspired to take many more slides, choosing them with a story in mind, as he does so well with his camera. My photos so far have been at random, single shots, determined by framing and subject.

John has offered me membership in a photographic group in Manila collecting material on various cultural groups here. That may turn into next summer's project. Through MSU I have privileged access to the Maranao, probably as mysterious to Manila because of their reputation as unconquered fighters, as are the Tasaday, the "forest people".

You should not worry about the situation here. Everyone in the American bureaucracy knows my name from the search for my body last summer, and if anything turns serious, they will take good care. As with the slide show, this declaration is, I think, mostly for impression. Life here will not greatly change.

I got the zoom lens ordered through my air force friend last week, a late birthday present to myself, just in time for shots taken this week with Gibb. The lens, 85-205, is wonderful for faces and transforms still photography into something with motion. Especially helpful for slides, where the zoom can properly frame the picture.

Just received more information on martial law. All transportation and communication facilities are under government control, a 7 pm to 6am curfew is in effect, public meetings are outlawed, schools have been closed. The provision that will affect us most is the last one. Just got home from a midnight meeting. Mostly conforming with the other provisions. There is a rumor that Israel has declared war.

Some faculty are saying the declaration is not such a bad idea if it will arrange the country around worthy goals. Perhaps that is for impression as well. Marcos delivered an hour-long speech tonight in English explaining his decision. 37 of 44 towns in Central Luzon are in NPA (New People's Army) control, he says, which probably means that farmers in those towns are selling, giving, their goods to the wrong army, instead of paying it in rent or taxes to the government or landlords. Such a tactic sounds more probable than the bombings that are rumored everywhere, but go against all schools of guerrilla warfare.

Mindanao will probably be the most interesting place to watch, because the Moslems here have the most effective organization for resistance, and it is here that Marcos will play his cards, reveal whether the threat and his response is genuine. Sending the Philippine Army here to collect guns would be NO JOKE.

If there is no trouble from Mindanao then his scheme is a show, a way to avoid the election of '73, by convincing people in the north that there is trouble in the south, convincing those in the south that there is insurrection in the north, and that is most likely.

I will send this note with Mr. Gibb to Hong Kong where he can mail it, if he manages to get out of the country!

Martti Vallila

Letter 29 October 30

In times of martial law, teachers and soldiers reverse roles. It is now we who have nothing to do. Classes have been suspended for two weeks. No one knows when they will resume. Everyone has heard a rumor. My favorite is the one that says we've had our last classes of the semester. That would give me much time for my trip north, although I don't know where I will find the needed money.

I have taken advantage of the break. Last week I returned to Camiguin Island, and have decided that is one place you must see. You may remember my description from last year's trip: Paradise Island of sweet lansones and violent volcanoes, which I climbed. I am becoming so familiar a face that the people no longer call me "father".

I was there last fiesta time, in May. There happened to be a fiesta there last week, in the town of Sogay, although the mood was mooted and the dancing ended by 11 because of the curfew. A recent flood had placed many in a position from which they could not celebrate. Joe Bautista, the island's newspaperman still managed to guide me to three full tables of lechon (pig) between eight and eleven in the morning.

I was curious about the effects of martial law on that island. A few families own all its coconuts, and a strong free farmers movement has begun. They must be the communists that Marcos talks about. The day before I arrived, 16 had been arrested for harvesting without permission of the landlords, and paying them a share. Bond was set at P9000 each. That is many years of coconut harvesting. The case is in civil court, may well have been encouraged by the mood of the times.

The interview of Marcos on Meet the Press was printed in today's Daily Express, the only newspaper available these days. It is Marcos owned. The reporter's questions were more interesting than his answers. They asked what people here might do with western educations. We are made to understand things on the basis of half hour interviews covering all subjects, tied together with a string of words, words whose meanings people don't have the courage, or perhaps the curiosity, to examine. People assemble in front of TV cameras and reassure all by using the same words they have heard before.

I have a suspicion this country will be more and more in the news, and the time between now and the election, scheduled for '73 will be fascinating. The father of the family with whom I stay in Manila thinks of Marcos as a good man, trapped in a web of old customs, institutions. I am sure that he will now say that Marcos has the power to get rid of some.

Is Marcos in fact allied, in spirit, with the young students who have gone into the central Cagayan valley of Mindanao to organize farmers there, to convince them to no longer pay their land tax, the people he now describes, to the satisfaction of all, as communists? Is he in fact allied with those, they are the brightest students in the universities, IN SPIRIT, or has he, in office, grown far beyond questions of spirit, has he been reduced to questions of political pragmatism, survival? They may, in the end, lead in similar directions.

Many believe Marcos shut down the papers to give the proposed constitution a chance of passing. It is a collection of controversial proposals, on religion, marriage, land distribution, as well as government reform, and would be defeated if subjected to the scrutiny of a notoriously free press.

Now the Daily Express presents life in simple, and _good_ terms. Each day the front page carries a picture of a woman in the marketplace, fishermen, butchers in Manila, people doing ORDINARY things, as before. The caption is always "things are more peaceful, life continues, with more security."

Did he have those shots taken months ago? No. Scenes like that are everywhere, and he is probably right, probably because all are reading the Daily Express now. With such good press, the constitution has a good chance of being passed, bringing parliamentary government to the Philippines, and incidentally, only, allowing Marcos to continue as head of state!

If the PEOPLE demand it, he said on NBC, the PEOPLE, in the form of a parliament composed of the CONGRESS, present, the CONSTITUTIONAL CONVENTION that Marcos is rumored to control with payrolls. One delegate set off a scandal a couple of months ago by making public the contents of an envelope he had been given by Emilda Marcos. If those PEOPLE, none of them subject to election till '75, <u>demand</u> it, then he will remain. A popular term here is TUTA NI MARCOS meaning little puppy or lap dog.

In the Chinese history course we were discussing parallels between the Chinese situation in the early 20th century, when the emperor had been overthrown, and a "people's government", the Kuomintang, always speaking in the language of democracy, came to power, more or less from the top, never having been elected by anyone, persuaded foreign governments to recognize it, presumed it had the people's mandate, as well as the mandate of heaven, and was ultimately driven out because it never did make the grass roots connection, was always operating through landlord, the bureaucrat, failing to stop the strength of the evil.

Seven years ago Marcos was new, very popular, looked to with hope, so I am told. Soon after his reelection, the peso was devalued, and prices have spiraled since. He is no longer a folk hero, if folk, premarital law, are any indication. Perhaps he harbors the hope, the secret mission, and his tragedy is to have lost touch.

Last year's student body president, who is now trying to bring electricity, light, to the barrios between Iligan and Cagayan has told me that his most effective organizing tool, the idea to which most people in these small fishing villages gravitate is Philippine statehood! The folk hero in Mindanao, if there is one, is a combination of GI Joe to the old, who came in time of trouble, with chocolates, and Che whose picture many of the young have on their sweatshirts.

In Manila, things are different I am told. It is the old folks who have worked the soil, or fished the waters, and it is the young who go to Manila for jobs.

Who can Marcos ask to reform but those in government now? He has demanded the resignations of all government workers. The first to comply are those that deserve most to be rehired, perhaps. It is not an easy situation, and I honestly can't see a change in the big picture. He is successful, personally, in the short term. It is all very interesting.

The longer I stay here, the more I feel day to day life is a mix not only of the past, expressed historically by periods of Moslem, Spanish, American, Japanese, American rule, but in the present, with each of these things still alive, the first two very much alive in custom, in ritual, especially in the south, and the last alive here, in JUDGEMENT, in the western press, from the outside.

In the north the American influence has seeped into custom. A mix of standards. In America those proposing an alternative way lack a base, a tradition that has survived the vast power of the electronic instant. Here that is no problem. Available for the price of a boat ride, or the 10 centavos that a paper costs. If you are a city dweller you can probably afford the boat ticket, which is more expensive than the paper, all that is necessary for outside perspective in the barrio!

Eleven MSU students are still in the PC stockade just above downtown Marawi at Camp Kelley, the old American military station. They were taken from dormitories on the first night after the declaration, some because their names were on "the list", rumored to be 100 names long, others because they resented questions, and still others because their hair was too long.

They are now not greatly outnumbered by students on campus, for most have gone home. It will take at least three days for classes to begin, after any official opening. Colleges in large cities and provincial capitals will be last to resume. The trip north should give me good comparative material. So far all of Marcos' actions seem geared to the Manila area, and when the declarations, such as school closings, become nation-wide they appear awkward.

On Monday I visited Sultan Sochoya in Molando, across the lake, to observe the ceremony of the first night of Puasa or Ramadan, the Moslem month of fasting. While walking among the rice fields, students asked me why school was closed. It was hard to explain to someone who has never been to Manila. The people of Molando have turned in 10 long rifles, those in nearby Bayaboo say they will refuse to comply with the October 25 deadline.

Collection here is difficult because much of the merchandise is home made, and the Philippine Constabulary have no idea how to categorize them. Much of what is not home made is "imported". By the end of this month we should know how Marcos plans to deal with the Moslems. A very tricky situation.

Don't worry about me. Only danger is under work, and I am having no trouble filling idle moments.

Late news: some classes may be resumed on Monday, in agriculture, forestry, and engineering. I don't know about liberal arts. Members of KM, the radical organization, will be purged. "Maoist oriented professors" will be fired. I don't know what that means for someone who has been teaching Chinese history!

All but two of the students held in the stockade have been released, but the opening of classes on Monday will be limited, as most students are gone. Let me know if my birthday letter to Marja got through. It had some political comments in it. Some have been telling stories of the steaming of letters in the central post office.

***

It is perhaps providential that my last letter ended with that observation, or rumor. Soon after writing it I travelled north to the rice terraces of the Mountain Province. I observed the mountain people gather from their terraces for a weekly market that appeared on a field for the day. Goods were exchanged, there was much activity, and at the end of the day, the temporary town disappeared. After a week in the cool mountains I returned to Manila, feeling fatigued.

I thought my condition was due to the change in climate. I had no desire to drink a San Miguel or taste fried food. I was instinctively drawn to fresh fruits, mangoes. Welcomed into the home of a friend whose father was a doctor, my eyelids were pulled back to reveal serious jaundice. I had been urinating into the ground in the mountains, a place devoid of mirrors, so I was unaware of my condition.

I was told to go immediately to the hospital, admitted, and examined. I had a serious case of serum hepatitis. I remembered an injection of gamma globulin (to protect me from malaria) from a "sterilized" giant needle at the MSU health center. Immediate medication was rest. My body was not strong enough to accommodate some of the medicines that were given me later in the week. Once I received these medicines, worms of enormous size, killed by them, appeared in my stool. If I had been given the medication earlier, these worms would have been driven from my digestive system to other parts of my body, explained my doctor. Alcohol was out of the question. No fried foods. Fresh vegetables and fruits was the proscribed diet. Just as mother nature had told me.

When I had enough strength, I went to MSU, organized my belongings, and prepared my departure. I went to the health clinic to explain what had happened and was told:

"Oh, hepatitis. It happens all the time."

I flew to California from Hong Kong, via Alaska (allowing me to claim a presence in my 50th state). I remember the stewardess on the trans-Pacific flight asking me which of three entrees I wanted for my meal, and thinking how silly this choice seemed, from the perspective of the limited choices I had had for eighteen months in Mindanao. Any of them is fine, I answered.

I arrived at the Oakland airport without dollars. I had an American Express credit card and two cameras. I asked a taxi to take me to the nearest American Express office where I was told that the only way to get money from my card would be to write a check. When I explained that I was returning from eighteen months in the Philippines, I was politely told nothing was possible.

I went across the street to a bank. Nothing was possible there as well. What a contrast with the Philippines, where everything was possible, arranged through a web of human beings, sensitive to reasonable requests. The cab driver observed my visits to the offices, sensed my frustration. I had no option but to return with him to the airport. On the return trip I confided that I had no money with which to settle his $50 charge. I promised to pay him as soon as I got cash. I asked him where I could leave money for him. He pointed to the dispatcher and drove away.

I found a Western Union booth that was manned at the airport, called Rose and asked her to wire $200. It took about an hour for the authorization to arrive in Oakland. When it did the woman in the booth told me that I was lucky. Someone had wired funds from her location earlier in the day so there was $200 in her drawer that she could give me.

I went to the cabstand found the dispatcher and gave him $50. His amazement raised the question in my mind as to whether my driver would receive my payment. I had settled my obligation to the human web in Oakland. From Oakland I continued to Washington. It took me several months to regain my bearings physically, and considerably longer psychologically. I got the job on the Amtrak train to Montreal described earlier as a first reintroduction to American life.

I started speaking English in the American manner, submitted an article on the Maranao to the magazine of the American Museum of Natural History in New York that was rejected, visited the offices of National Geographic and saw some of my photos cropped on their modern equipment. None of this led to work.

Amtrak took me from DC to Seattle and eventually to Chicago where I now return in this exploration of near death experiences after a chapter on the implications of what I learned in the Philippines on the pressing issue of the day: radical Islamic terror.

Islamic teachings

One of the central questions posed at the start of the 21st century is whether Islam is a religion of peace or whether its teachings justify, even encourage, violence. I am no Islamic scholar but you don't need to be one to form an opinion on the subject.

Many have had their thoughts on the topic formed by the media they watch or listen to. There seems to be a political divide: Democrats parrot Obama's mantra that Islam is a religion of peace. Republicans point to motivations having to do with meeting virgins in heaven as explanations for shocking acts of terror. The division of opinion is not strictly along party lines but the pattern described cannot be denied.

My experiences in Mindanao and the Sulus can, in retrospect, be considered "field work" on the subject. I offer here conclusions I have drawn forty years after experiencing the near death experiences described in the previous chapter, hoping they may inform current debate in a useful way. I pose some of the key questions in the debate and answer them from a perspective that is a combination of youthful experience and subsequent years in the world of hard knocks.

The first issue is the role of Islam in a society. Does Islam recognize a distinction between religion and the state? The answer is no. In Islam the religion IS the state. Sharia Law governs man's (and woman's) behavior. Period. Praying five times a day is one manifestation of the hold the religion has on its believers. Islam preaches a direct relationship between man and God without intermediaries, like Jesus (considered a false prophet). I saw evidence of this everywhere in Moslem Mindanao.

I also saw a devotion to Christianity in the Philippines among its believers that was new to my eyes. With not much to distract from a pursuit of food and sex life on the islands was simple.

The next question is whether Moslems are ready to fight to the death against infidels. The answer to this question is yes. The "juramentado", whose sabre-wielding charges against warriors armed with modern weapons resulted in the invention of the Colt 45, a weapon designed to have sufficient power to knock a man backwards, is testimony to the ferocity with which Islamic fighters attacked their foes. There was no thought of survival in their world.

Another key question: are Moslems able to accept cohabitation with Christians? The existence of Mindanao State University was testimony to the Philippine government's desire to answer this question in the affirmative. I was honored to be a participant in a social experiment of such audacity and importance. I saw difficulties of the attempt up close. The preparation of Moslem and Christian students was so different. The Maranao kids had gone to "ghost schools" in the villages. The Christian kids were at MSU on scholarships won in competitions. I did not see much interaction between the two communities of students. The killing of the Bahai students from Indonesia (see page 142) was evidence of a willingness to kill infidels.

I have seen Moslems and Christians live in peace in Tatarstan, Russia and Turkey. In the Philippines the two communities lived separately, the Moslems in self-imposed enclaves. Wealthy Maranao, like president Tamano of MSU, were able to operate in both worlds but few Christians were invited into Maranao society.

The Maranao way of life was under threat. A people who once ruled the huge island, whose ancient beliefs had been merged with Islam, as evidenced in "lalang", the "high language" in which the story that tied their ancestors to Mecca was told at funerals, found themselves isolated in the hills. The Tausug, a sea people who were similarly converted to Islam and once ruled the Sulu Sea, were clinging to footholds on the islands.

Modern life was changing traditional ways throughout the islands. The question that needs now to be asked: is the expansion of Islam threatening *our* way of life? Are we being transformed into people living in fear?

The question Winston Churchill posed, in 1925, in his essay "Shall we all commit suicide?" was inspired by his insight that modern man would soon be equipped with technologies able to destroy the planet. We have managed to navigate our way into the 21st century by developing and using international organizations Churchill was hoping would be up to the task. He believed that effective and inspired leadership was essential.

Key to this strategy continuing to work is cooperation between Russia and America. That is the game I am in, sure that cooperation in technology commercialization is a key fiber of a rope tying the two countries together that must hold and be further strengthened. Current events point in discouraging directions.

A new threat has emerged. Terror, in the name of Islam, has entered the world's consciousness. Images on TV and the Internet of beheadings have awoken the world to a reality that some do not want to acknowledge. The protection provided for years by a doctrine of "mutually assured destruction" that kept the world's nuclear powers from unleashing their capabilities is irrelevant in this new, "politically correct" world. What if the enemy belongs to no state? What if the enemy's state of mind is suicidal?

In an essay following the one mentioned above (in his book "Thoughts and Adventures") Churchill muses about "mass effects in modern life" on man's psychology. As we have become economically developed most people have become elements of some bigger entity, as Churchill puts it:

"We are witnessing a great diminution in the number of independent people who had some standing of their own, albeit a small one, and who if they conducted their affairs with reasonable prudence could 'live by no man's leave underneath the law'. They may be better off as the salaried officials of great corporations; but they have lost in forethought, in initiative, in contrivance, in freedom and in effective civil status."

Churchill was both a believer in the "great man" theory of history and one of that theory's acknowledged practitioners. He saw clearly the threats Hitler and Stalin represented to the advancement of civilization and freedom.

Has this "tendency to mass effects and the suppression of the individual" rid the modern world of characters needed to *lead* humanity forward? To *prevent* catastrophe?

Does the western world have the inner strength and confidence (in its own institutions and history) to confront a radical version of Islam that is overrunning large swaths of the Middle East and sending swarms of refugees into exile? The battle is being fought in social media. Victory requires clear-sighted leadership and the courage to speak truth.

The south side of Chicago

As previously explained I was given the south side of Chicago as my sales territory when transferred by Amtrak to Chicago from Seattle. Amtrak put me up in the Pick Congress Hotel on the lakefront not far from the white Santa Fe building where the Amtrak sales offices were located. I noticed what I thought was a bullet hole in the wall of the hotel room in which I spent my first night in Chicago.

The south side of Chicago is one of America's main killing fields, home to gang violence that produces death statistics that dwarf those of LA and New York. It is where the Nation of Islam's Elijah Muhammad lived and where Barack Obama served as a community organizer. In 1974 I drove that territory in my Mustang convertible with little concern.

My memories of Chicago are connected with my marriage to Dominique in the chapel in the middle of the University of Chicago's south side campus, the natural delivery of our two daughters in a birthing center on the north side, and the start of my serious business career, not death.

I arrived in this great inland city by rail, as a wandering adventurer, and left it eight years later for the big apple on a jet plane, a successful IBMer with an MBA from one of America's top business schools, ready to take on the world. Stanford had opened my mind to the wonders of the west coast and western civilization. The University of Chicago taught me how to think. Stanford provided me a path to Asia, the U of C got me into the big leagues of American business.

The birthing center housed in Illinois Masonic Hospital was not far from the north side apartment Dominique and I occupied on Surf Street and an acceptable compromise between the home birth Dominique imagined and the operating room she wanted nothing to do with. I was an observer more than a participant at each birth, providing as much encouragement as I could during moments I will never forget. Dominique brought Sofia home to an awaiting Kristine after only a day in the hospital, shocking our neighbors. Kristine was ready to play with her sister immediately. It took a couple of years for Sofia to achieve the status of a playmate. Once that happened the two sisters became inseparable best friends, destined to marry best friends (in Boston)!

The professional rebirth I experienced in Chicago was thanks to the university. I got into the U of C MBA program unaware of its reputation. The fact I could get an MBA there at night, while working, and have my employer pay, was the key to this life-changing choice. During my first quarter, paid by Amtrak, I asked for the placement office's help in finding work with a company more involved in international business than my current employer. Richard Thain, director of the placement office, circulated a resume he helped me develop to companies that included IBM. I was interviewed by a marketing manager in the tall black IBM building in downtown and given a thirty-minute test that must have identified sufficient potential to warrant acceptance into a training program that lasted a year and was a perfect complement to the formal "Chicago school" training I was getting at night.

I suppose that working full time while going through a night MBA program and having a first child qualifies as a "near death" experience for a couple. (Kristine was two months old when I got my degree in Rockefeller Chapel.)

My closest "near death" experience of a more classic sort was probably the winter day when my Mustang did a 360 on a bridge over the Chicago River covered with an invisible sheet of ice. I was alone. It was late. If a car or truck had been coming from the other direction there was nothing I could have done to prevent impact and its consequences.

My sales calls on the south side headquarters of Muhammad Speaks, the weekly newspaper of the Nation of

Islam, to sell them on Amtrak's package express program gave me a taste of the gun culture of south Chicago. Before being allowed into the building where the paper was published I was frisked for weapons. I managed to get some business from the Nation of Islam. Several cities to which they sent bundles of papers weekly were on Amtrak routes and package express fares were lower than what truckers were charging.

This success, for which I received no payment, made me enemies among the baggage handlers of Union Station. I was giving them lots of additional work! I learned that the measure of success in a government job is not to rock the boat while pleasing your boss. I had a sales job without any commission. The only payment for the initiatives I was taking were the experiences these initiatives provided me. (What a different world I entered with IBM where performance against quotas was measured, and determined whether one stayed in a job, was promoted to another, or fired.)

Not only did my south side territory contain a wholesaler of ski packages (leading to adventures described in a previous chapter) and the headquarters of Muhammad Speaks, it was also home to the world famous Chicago Symphony Orchestra. Orchestra Hall was on Michigan Avenue, just down the street from the Amtrak ticket office. Ten times each year the Symphony took a special train to Milwaukee for concerts there. I got into the habit of joining the orchestra on these trips. My reward was a back stage look at a concert and a chance to meet the musicians.

Conductor George Solti kept his distance. I was welcomed into a group that played cards on the train and ate dinner at Mader's, a German restaurant in Milwaukee, prior to the concerts. A prominent member of that group was cellist Frank Miller, considered by many as the greatest living cello player. He insisted on carrying his instrument with him, not trusting it to the baggage car. I made a friend of Carl Fasshauer, manager of the orchestra, and was invited back stage to performances at Orchestra Hall in Chicago.

Unforgettable memories of Orchestra Hall include seeing Vladimir Horowitz and Arthur Rubinstein on their last visits to Chicago, up close, and witnessing a performance of Richard Strauss' Salome (an operatic masterpiece that climaxes with the beheading of John the Baptist) sung by Leontyne Price and Martti Talvela that I consider the greatest artistic act it has been my fortune to witness. The Chicago Tribune's review of that performance in the morning paper confirmed that those present had experienced a unique moment.

My predecessors on the Symphony account had taken little interest in their special customer. A ticket for the "special train", issued by the Amtrak ticket office on Michigan Avenue, needed to be taken to Union Station and given to the conductor who would accompany the train. The Milwaukee performances were always on Mondays. One of those Mondays followed the Sunday when time was "sprung" forward by an hour. I did not wearing a watch in those days, relying on public clocks to keep me on time.

I remember arriving at Union Station in what I considered plenty of time and being shocked to learn that the train had left. Without a ticket! I had been tricked and confused by clocks in the street that had not been "sprung forward". I scrambled to find the next train going to Milwaukee and got there just in time to join my friends for dinner and was able to settle matters with the conductor on the trip back. (Was my lackadaisical attitude towards time a reaction to the lack of urgency in my job? I got into the habit of wearing a watch when working for IBM.)

***

I spent my only night in jail not on the south side of Chicago but in the swanky neighborhood of Willamette. For a reason I do not now recall I was in the northern suburb, not in my territory, one Friday afternoon calling on travel agents there when I was informed by Lydia Scuderi, owner of a travel agency employing six young women, that the social event of the season, the black and white ball, was taking place that evening. Her girls needed an escort. Would I be interested? Of course! There was one hitch. I would have to go dressed in black and white, and the suit I had on was beige. No problem. Lydia offered to take me home and fit me into one of her husband's tuxedos if I agreed to get to her house around six. I saw no problem.

When I arrived Lydia gave me a gin and tonic and addressed the challenge we needed to solve. Her husband's waistline was considerably larger than mine. The length of the tuxedo pants was fine but several safety pins was needed to attach the pants in the back so as to prevent them from falling off. She managed this with Germanic efficiency.

We were off to the garden party where I did my best to amuse her girls, and myself, with food, dance and drink. Before I knew it it was 2am. Time to drive home to Chicago. Stanford was playing Illinois in football in Champaign on Saturday and I was planning on taking an early morning train there. (One of the main benefits of working for Amtrak was free rail travel anywhere in the US.) I was unfamiliar with the swanky neighborhood, knowing only that I needed to find the freeway going south. At a stop sign I made a right turn without coming to a full stop, according to the police officer who appeared out of nowhere with his red flashing siren.

I could not imagine what I had done wrong and told him so, explained that I was on my way back to Chicago, it was two in the morning and even if I had not come to a complete stop I didn't see the great danger of that. He asked me whether I had a bond card. I asked him what that was. Something an insurance company provides that serves as a substitute for the $100 he would otherwise need from me in cash, he explained. I had neither a bond card nor the necessary cash. I needed access to a bank to get funds. My only alternative was to spend the night in jail, he explained. I could visit a bank in the morning. What could I say or do?

I slept off my hangover in my borrowed tuxedo, alone, in the cell of one of the wealthiest suburbs of Chicago. The next morning I was able to withdraw the funds needed to post bond. I missed the football game, returned the tuxedo to Lydia, and made a court appearance a month later in which the judge credited me with time served and did not ask for any more money. I considered the experience a rather benign introduction to the prison system. (If my jail time had been on the south side I imagine my recollections might be quite different.)

This experience allows me to occasionally start a conversation with the question of "have you ever been in prison?" as an alternative to "have you ever had a near death experience?"

***

My days at IBM did not include many "near death" experiences of the physical sort. At the start of every year I was given a quota that needed to be met to achieve the 100% Cub. Failure to do so was a "near death" experience of the business sort. The most immediate difference I noticed between Amtrak and IBM was the alignment of forces and objectives in the latter. Not only did I have my quota but my manager had his quota, which was the sum total of the quotas he distributed to his sales team. The manager's success was thus directly linked to the success of each member of his (or her) sales team.

An independent operator by nature, I was comfortable being left alone, asking occasionally for help navigating IBM's internal systems if any parts of the "IBM iceberg" (the support network that could be called upon) were needed to close a deal. At Amtrak independence and initiative were seen as threats. The games there were political and territorial. Managers focused on protecting whatever position in the bureaucracy they occupied from attack from below. There were no sales quotas, no measurement of performance.

Each year roughly seventy percent of IBM's salespeople made the 100% club. Those that didn't were given another year to recover. If they couldn't they were asked to consider different work, sometimes as a systems engineer or administrator within the company. More elusive that a 100% Club was the "Golden Circle", reserved for top performers. Making the circle required not only effort, but luck. Reward was a more exotic location, Bermuda in my case, and the right to bring a spouse along. I had taken my family to 100% Club locations at my cost in previous years, so that part of the recognition was an additional financial reward.

Making the circle in my final year on quota helped get me to New York where I took first steps of an international business career, my objective from the start. It was in international travel that I came closest to "near death experiences" while at IBM. During a visit to Amsterdam I was confronted, one evening, by a knife-wielding man, who appeared suddenly out of the dark. I told him I did not have any money on me, which was true. I did not even have my passport, as that had been picked from my pocket earlier during the same trip! Note: beware of Amsterdam.

The loss of my passport presented real difficulties. I was on my way to South Africa to get clarification from top executives there on what made the South African character set special. My job at the time was to negotiate support for special character sets in IBM word processing products. Getting a replacement US passport and a replacement visa required going to the Hague, the location of all embassies in the Netherlands, which I managed to do in a rental car. I got replacements in time to make my flight to Johannesburg, via Nairobi, on KLM. Landing in "Joberg" in 1984 was like dropping into a surreal, temporary calm.

The meeting at the top floor of the tower occupied by IBM was my first surreal moment. Around the table sat twelve IBMers, all Englishmen. Not a single speaker of

Afrikaan, the special language I was there to ask questions about. They summoned a lower level employee to answer my basic question: what made the South African character set special?

The answer astonished me. The South African keyboard featured a script "L" instead of a lower case "l" to designate liter, as was the case in the rest of Europe. The second "special character" was the combination of two letters on a single key, "'n", to represent a much used abbreviation in the Afrikaan language. It looked to me to be a case of self-imposed isolation, symptomatic of the situation in South Africa at the time. Printing the apostrophe "'" and then an "n" on a Displaywriter (the IBM product we were discussing) proved to be a better treatment of South Africa's special requirement then forcing the combination to be printed by a "special character", in which case the end product was difficult to read.

My impression of South Africa's isolation was cemented during my visit to Pretoria where I visited the Voortrekker monument, consisting of a marble frieze (the largest in the world) depicting a circling of wagons and battles fought between Dutch explorers and African tribes surrounding them. The hotel I stayed in served both blacks and whites but I saw no tables in the cocktail lounge that had a mix of races. I could not imagine how South Africa would escape a "near death experience" it seemed to face in 1984. (How Nelson Mandela and F. W. de Klerk managed to negotiate a peaceful transition in a country that appeared headed for civil war is a tribute to both.) My return flight to Europe, on South African Airlines, headed in the direction of water, after a quick stop in Namibia, because it was not allowed to fly over African air space.

Johannesburg remains one of the world's most dangerous places, like the south side of Chicago.

***

My most serious "near death" experience while with IBM was the spiritual death I experienced when transferred from

European headquarters in Tour Pascal, overlooking Paris, to the windowless offices in Raleigh housing the staff of the global network support office.

In my opinion IBM was not leveraging its position as the world's first truly global company. Founder Tom Watson's vision of building autonomous operations in nations across the globe was executed so successfully that IBM country managers considered themselves chiefs of their own domains. This independent thinking, important to the success of the company when it was pioneering data processing, created barriers to addressing opportunities brought on by globalization.

Revenue from "services" was growing much faster than revenue from the sale of hardware. IBM was in a position to help the world's biggest companies "globalize" their operations. They were all IBM customers. They needed help dealing with numerous telecom carriers. Telecoms were government organizations, many in the midst of re-organization. IBM was the only company in a position of strength everywhere. How IBM solved its internal communications challenges could offer trusted, revenue generating guidance to others. But IBM's internal systems were fraught with tension.

I saw this tension play out at European headquarters. Each country operation defended its autonomy and resisted direction from the center. There was no central decision making authority in the company. Telecommunications was viewed within IBM as a side business, like software and services. This myopia was ultimately corrected by Louis Gerstner years later when he shifted the company's focus from hardware to services but IBM went through its own "near death experience" before that happened.

***

During my Raleigh days one of my co-workers, Jack, experienced the tragic loss of his son in a traffic accident. The funeral was attended not only by most students in his high school but by hundreds of IBMers. Jack and his son were golfing buddies. Jack Jr.'s death was a blow from which his father never recovered. It was a reminder to all of how swiftly, and unexpectedly, death can come. My closest brush with death on the road was on the day after one of the happiest days of my life, 7/7/07, the day on which Kristine was married in Weston, outside of Boston, to Alex in an outdoor ceremony allowed by mother nature as threatening clouds held back.

Twenty-four hours later Dominique and I were driving in a rainstorm on Route 128 not far from the hotel where the wedding party had stayed. I was driving a small Miata convertible borrowed from Alain, a friend who needed someone to take care of his car during a trip to China of undetermined length. Dominique and I were remarking how lucky Kristine and Alex had been with the weather. If the wedding had been a day later, it would have been forced indoors by the downpour we were driving through.

We were in the right lane passing a truck to our left. The truck's wheels were spraying water in our direction. I pushed on the gas to accelerate us past the monster. At that instant the truck swerved into our lane. The spinning bolts of the massive right front tire chewed into the rear left side of the Miata pushing us off the road. I instinctively turned the steering wheel hard left to keep us going forward as we screeched to a stop. I couldn't imagine why the driver had turned into us. The reason was simple. He had no idea we were there, in his blind spot, at the moment he decided to switch lanes. He was as surprised at the sudden contact as we were, though his truck was hardly affected.

We skidded to a stop on the gravel. The truck slowed down and pulled over in front of us. I got out shaking, looked at the mess around our car's tire. The tire was not flat, had miraculously not been punctured by the twisted steel around it. I found a young driver in the cab of the truck nervously calling his boss on a cell phone. When he connected I asked to speak with the man who requested that I not report the accident to insurance. He would take care of any repairs to my car at a shop he knew in New Hampshire and rent me a car for the time it would take to get it fixed. I saw no reason not to accept his offer.

I wanted to flag down a police car and get a report of the accident on the record. At least two police cars passed us without stopping. The officer who finally did seemed reluctant to put anything in writing. I found this reaction strange and spent as much time on it as I did on the accident when telling of our "near death experience" later to the kids. The Miata was repaired in two days and the paint job almost matched the rest of the body. Alain noticed the difference when he saw the car six months later and I told him the story.

Passing through New York

Departing Chicago for New York on a temporary two-year assignment to the world trade organization may have been the way IBM officially viewed my transfer. In my mind my exit was permanent. I was leaving the domestic part of IBM to pursue my dream of international business. I had no idea how my goal would be reached but was certain that returning to Chicago as a marketing manager, the next step in the typical career path, was not in my cards.

The move to New York involved a major financial step. In Chicago Dominique and I had been tenants, in three Surf Street apartments, two in the same building, a third in a larger unit across the street that we moved into once Sofia was born. In New York we made our plunge into home ownership. I had made good money during my years on quota in Chicago so I had enough for a down payment on a house.

My problem was that moving to a staff involved a significant reduction in salary. As my assignment to New York was temporary my salary was augmented with the payment of a per-diem which I was able to show to the bank as part of my compensation, or cash flow. I was not in the market for a place on 5th avenue, as Dominique hoped. That was where the French consulate was located. Instead I shopped around in Connecticut. My office was in White Plains so we would be living, for the first time in my life, the suburban life.

The Merrill Lynch agent introduced to us by IBM asked how much I could spend and opened the listing catalogue to pages at the upper end of the range I mentioned. I was more interested in looking at properties at the lower end. One looked affordable and had considerable upside potential: a converted horse barn on a secluded piece of property in Stamford with a small river in the back. It was perfect for the kids who were at an age where a back yard was important. We had more than a back yard. We had a private, grassy play area boarded by a forest and a river. To say that the house needed work was an understatement. I considered it a perfect place to test my skills at demolition. The place needed to be opened up. A second roof had been built above a lower one. If the lower roof was removed, and skylights placed in the upper one, a dark structure would be converted into a spacious one!

    I visualized it in my mind's eye and set about making it happen. I had no idea that I was training myself for more serious renovations, years later, in San Francisco. During the eighteen months I spent in New York, before being transferred to Paris, I transformed the former horse barn into a property that I was able to rent for an amount that covered the mortgage when we moved to Paris, and was able to sell for twice what I paid for it when it was time to return to the US.

    I benefitted, for the first time, from a run up in real estate prices and fortunate timing when I needed to sell. Able to buy the place with a down payment of around $20,000 and able to carry it for five years, partially with payments from tenants, I made over $125,000 when the place sold for $250,000. The lessons I learned from this experience in real estate was the importance of making the conversion from tenant to owner as soon as I was able to afford it, the value of sweat equity in bringing out a property's potential, and the role that timing and luck play in the eventual evaluation of the investment.

    In the only spring that we inhabited the house the region experienced rainfalls that converted the small stream in our back yard into a river that flooded our property. That was not our first issue with respect to water and the Connecticut property. The property was listed as being serviced by water from a well in the back yard. Rose advised that I have the quality of the water tested, as a contingency, when finalizing my offer to purchase. This proved to be very sound advice. The well was a shallow one, contaminated with bacteria that the tester hired by Merrill Lynch attempted to bring to within acceptable levels for the purpose of passing a water quality test. When requesting an independent assessment of the well I stumbled onto the same company that had been used by Merrill Lynch and they admitted to having poured significant amounts of chemicals into the water to get results that were legally acceptable. This revelation resulted in the digging of a deep well, at Merrill Lynch's expanse, prior to closing.

We survived both water incidents and I vowed never again to buy a home near running water. My dream house at the top of the hill on Vallejo Street was the polar opposite of my Connecticut farmhouse. In between we owned a home in Raleigh in which our daughters grew up. I made rather dramatic renovations to the North Carolina property as well, this time hiring professionals to install skylights and a second bathroom that allowed the house to expand along with our needs.

My initial leap into real estate occurred in New York and just as my stay in Paris reengineered me physically, our brief stay in the outskirts of New York revitalized my financial posture, providing me with funds which I would use to purchase the house in North Carolina and, later, the dream house in San Francisco.

There was another benefit from these renovations. I find office work frustrating in its abstractness and lack of immediate results. Physical work renovating properties on weekends and after work is psychologically rewarding. I find the act of demolition particularly gratifying. I have discovered that it is best to wait until a structure is taken apart before making final decisions on how the interior should be reshaped.

In my view renovation is an iterative process during which it is important to maintain flexibility. This approach runs counter to the process imposed by the permission givers who must be consulted and whose approval is needed.

Any chapter on New York should mention Broadway and show biz. Two stories emerge. A special bond developed between Rose and Kristine, her first grandchild. I believe the happiest days of Rose's life were the days she spent with Kristine, an ebullient child. Rose gave her the record of the musical Annie, which Kristine loved. As a third birthday present Rose wanted to treat Kristine to a New York weekend, first class, the highlight of which was a visit to see Annie on Broadway. She made reservations in the St. Regis Hotel and in the middle of the first row at the theater. It was the first Broadway show for me, for Rose and for Kristine who, for weeks afterwards, asked that the Annie record be played as she sang the ending of her favorite song "and tomorrow is only a day away!"

Our Stamford neighbor gave us tickets to the Radio City Music Hall Christmas show. Our four tickets were not in the front row but close enough for a great view. Two and a half year old Sofia was enchanted with the Rockettes and their red outfits. She stood up in her chair to get a better view. Sofia had a habit of standing still and placing the second and third fingers in her mouth while observing whatever held her attention. (It took her longer than usual to start talking, leading us to wonder if something was wrong. There was nothing wrong. When Sofia started talking it was in sentences.) The grand finale of the Christmas show brought the entire cast on stage, including a live camel, at which point I heard Sofia, standing next to me, say to herself, "j'ai jamais vu cas!" (I have never seen that!)

***

Professionally I was able to use the time in White Plains to build expertise in a rather esoteric area, the need to fully support the full character sets of European and Middle Eastern languages. These language requirements were often the only unique demands placed on developers of products on behalf of EMEA customers.

I was asked to conduct internal sessions on the subject to others in the EMEA White Plains product management organization once I learned the details of the requirements from country experts. Watching specialists representing the various European countries in a meeting was instructive.

The Germans and Austrians were in agreement and precise. Getting a straight answer from an Italian was difficult. My notes sent to Finland were always responded to in the Finnish language. I had to send notes back explaining that I did not speak the language of my father. This expertise got me the job in Paris when IBM reorganized and an Areas Division was created that included most of the countries that spoke the languages with special character requirements.

Russia, my muse

I was ready to experience some form of resurrection after years in the telecommunications wilderness of IBM when, on a whim, I visited Russia in the summer of 1991 at the moment the Soviet Union was collapsing. My frustration with the global network support office made the "leap of faith" inspired by that trip easy.

Russia is a country easily associated with "near death experiences" in the public imagination. The Soviet Union had a "death experience" in 1991. Vladimir Putin may be wishing for its resurrection but there is no denying that 1991 represented a watershed, the formal end of the USSR.

I have described my efforts to participate in the direction a "new Russia" takes in my other "Bannana books". Those books describe my travels, over more than twenty years, to the far reaches of the world's largest country, during its transition into a new world. The truth is that I experienced very few "near death experiences" of the physical sort in all of this time.

I felt safer traveling in Russia than I have in parts of Europe or the United States. The only moment I was confronted with violence was in the most public of places in Russia, just outside Red Square, in Moscow, in broad daylight. I had just arrived from Helsinki by train. My friend Nick picked me up at the station and drove me to a new hotel (the Moscova, my preferred hotel overlooking Red Square, was closed for renovation and I had not yet discovered Victoria House, the place that would become my regular Moscow location) where I had just enough time to register and drop my luggage, before driving me downtown.

I take cash to Russia, given the difficulty of accessing money machines, the reluctance of most places to accept credit cards, and the ubiquity of money changing booths. I leave most of my cash in my hotel room, taking only amounts I expect to change into rubles with me. This one time, I broke my rule.

The short visit to my hotel room did not give me time to transfer the euros I had brought with me into my secured luggage. They remained in the flap of my day planner. I had a rather thick bundle of small bills, obtained from cash machines in Helsinki that spit out 50 and 20 euro notes. Nick dropped me off near Red Square at my request. I had errands to run in the neighborhood. I was a bit fatigued from my night on the train and jet lag, having arrived recently from the US, but reasonably alert. Carrying only my computer case I bought an ice cream with a few rubles left over from my previous visit.

Carrying the ice cream in one hand I walked near General Zukov's statue facing the renovating Moscova Hotel and was climbing the stairs to the park above the Manège shopping area when I was approached by a man with a swarthy completion who opened his coat showing me dollar bills asked me if I wanted to change money.

"Not interested, no" I answered and moved on to find a seat on a slab of red marble surrounding the park where I could finish my treat. Moments later I was approached again by the man and a companion. I waived him off taking my day planner out of the breast pocket of my jacket for a reason I do not understand. He spied the money inside. Like an animal he grabbed it from my hand. The planner flew into the air scattering euros which he and his friend, and I, began collecting. In a moment the two men disappeared into the crowd. All of this had occurred in an instant in the middle of passersby who seemed to pay little attention.

I was dumbfounded by my stupidity and terrible luck. The one time I am in public with significant amounts of cash is the one time I am approached in Red Square and robbed! I recalled the look in the man's face when he saw the euros. It was the look of an animal locked onto a meal. I collected my thoughts. What to do? I looked for a police station where I could report the incident. Looked inside the Manège with no luck and went into the metro station nearby where there was a small police office. I tried to explain what had happened, in English, to officers evidently not familiar with the language. They brought out forms in Russian motioning that I would have to fill them in, in Russian, paying a translator to do it. What was the point? My assailants were long gone. I took a deep breath and decided to move on.

I have had my pocket picked of cell phones and small amounts of cash on several occasions. It has happened in train stations in Moscow and St. Petersburg, and in Internet cafes in St. Petersburg and Novosibirsk, and once in the Cantina, my favorite bar in Moscow, as recounted in "Bannana in Russia". That theft also involved a passport and led to hilarious complications described in the travel chapter.

I am quite certain the FSB has developed an extensive file on my activities. This guess is informed by the fact that Serguei Simonov, my good friend and guide in Siberia, told me that he was questioned following each of my visits to Akademgorodok. I am surely a spy in the eyes of the FSB. No one could possibly be pursuing my activities alone.

I am no James Bond. I am following a calling informed by a particular personal history, living life on the edge, staying a step ahead of "near death experiences" described here.

The only serious "near death experiences" connected with Russia have been in the financial realm, where the non compliance with obligations detailed in written agreements on the part of Russian partners has necessitated legal actions described in my other "Bannana books". I have been forced to operate on the edge of financial ruin, to sell my properties in Finland and the US to keep my quest alive.

My business model for the commercialization of Russian technologies begins with the establishment of a company outside of Russia, in a country with a legal system that can be trusted to protect the interests of investors and provide credible technical validation of claims made on behalf of the Russian technology.

Finland was my first choice given my ties to the country and its reputation as a "squeaky clean", transparent, high tech nation.

Fleeing Finland

I have left Finland forever twice. First, in 1956 to come to America and a second time, in 2015, as a convicted embezzler owing over a half million euro! How and why the Supreme Court of Finland refused to consider appeals of absurd verdicts in both civil and criminal trials is explained in "Bannana's Crime and Punishment; 'Justice' in Finland".

Those debts constitute a "near death" not only of the financial kind but also, in my eyes, the death of sisu, a spirit of risk taking that I long associated with Finland, personified by its crazy ski jumpers. My financial execution was administered by Finns transformed into schizophrenics, ready to play the role of lap dogs to Russian money while most of the country detests and fears Russia. Most Finns have never visited their huge neighbor. "Don't go there without a rifle" is advice I have often heard.

Many of the Finns who have travelled to Russia have limited their experience to weekend drinking visits to St. Petersburg. Perhaps Finnish leaders long for the "good old days" when high-powered Finns met with high-powered Soviets and all was arranged behind closed doors. Those days are gone. Finnish lawyers working for Russian money attempted to finish me off in a legal system whose language I did not speak. I am done with the country of my father, a diplomat responsible for some of Finland's economic resurgence following the war.

***

I was unprepared for the reception I received in Finland and admit that I have faced my most serious financial "near death" experiences in my father's country. No good deed goes unpunished!

Innovation is a "bottom up" process based on the cultivation of brilliant ideas born in the garages of Silicon Valley, to site an archetype that other regions and nations are attempting to duplicate. Telecommunication technologies have rendered location less relevant than it was when key factors in the Bay Area created conditions that ignited the creative forces of the region. Globalization is today's reality, to which Silicon Valley is adapting, with the establishment of satellite operations in multiple regions of the globe. What is Finland's area of comparative advantage in the evolving innovation ecosystem?

I have argued in my other books and in a report submitted to the government of Finland that Finland's comparative advantage lies in its geographic and historical ties to its giant neighbor, Russia, a new country whose birth I have witnessed up close. An innovation-supporting ecosystem is developing, from the "bottom up", in Russia, evidenced by the emergence of venture fairs throughout the country and the growth of organizations such as Albina Nikkonen's Russian Venture Capital Association (RVCA) and Kendrick White's Marchmont Capital Partners, sponsors of such fairs. It has been my privilege and honor to speak at many of these fairs.

I have argued that because of its isolated, insulated history, with all technology considered a potential asset in a Cold War, there are insights still hidden in Russia awaiting proper conditions to be launched into the global marketplace. I have put my money and energy behind finding such technologies, protecting them with western patents and then assigned those patents to companies outside of the Russian "black box", somewhere the technologies can be validated, and investors and industrial partners can be attracted into necessary partnerships.

My efforts have gained the trust of Russian inventors, most notably that of Igor Pomytkin, inventor of a new and promising treatment and prevention of Alzheimer's disease. Details of how I met Dr. Pomytkin are in "Bannana in Russia". He accepted my premise that "Finland has what Russia needs". After forming a Finnish company, Buddha Biopharma Oy, we proceeded to have work done by Pomytkin on mice and rats in Russia replicated and expanded by specialists in Kuopio, Finland's medical city. Results were astonishingly encouraging.

The Finnish "Russian stigma" kicked in when I applied for financial support from Tekes, the agency responsible for funding promising Finnish startups (with a stated priority on its website on anything to do with "human wellness" which presumably includes Alzheimer's from which more than five million Finns suffer). Tekes turned down two applications from Buddha Biopharma. This led to my firing and the decision of my Russian "partners" to move their work out of Finland.

Buddha Biopharma was a Finnish company consisting of two Russians and a Finn who does not speak the language. Was this a reason to refuse funding? After top specialists in the country had agreed that Pomytkin's groundbreaking science in neuronal insulin resistance represented a basis for new fields of research and many high paying jobs? The reason given, in Finnish, was "lack of a sufficient business case!" Absurd. A monkey could make a business case for an effective treatment of Alzheimer's. (The ones submitted to Tekes in our applications are included in the appendix of "Bannana's Crime and Punishment.")

Finnish lawyers attempted to finish me off in a legal system whose language I do not understand by employing what I call a "motti strategy" in honor of tactics employed by the Finns in the Winter War of drawing their enemy, the Russians, deep into unfamiliar territory, isolating them in pockets ("motti") where they were slowly finished off by snipers or the weather.

My firing from Buddha Biopharma forced me to launch an arbitration in the Finnish Chamber of Commerce. My former "partners" responded by initiating a criminal investigation and charging me with the "crime" of paying myself a salary. The Swedish arbitrator's absurd award took away the 10% equity stake I had in the company, and saddled me with the legal costs of the Finnish assassins hired by my Russian "partners".

Not a pretty picture, a struggle for nothing less than my professional reputation and financial well-being, that I continue. My real "crime": not speaking the Finnish language and having the audacity to propose to Finland a "success story" with the potential to change the nature of the "top down" relationship "public servants" currently have with Russian counterparts to one based on "bottom up" innovation.

I admit to having an upside down view of the innovation process. When approaching funding organizations I believe I am doing *them* a favor by bringing them opportunities, not approaching them as a supplicant, grateful for any of their time spent in evaluating proposals and listening to mumbo jumbo about how the proposals are inadequate, how more information is needed...

I am certain I was doing Finland a service by convincing Pomytkin and Verteletsky to support the establishment of a company there. Pomytkin was looking for somewhere he could continue his research. Working inside Russia was complicated by the difficulty of getting anything through customs. Kuopio has the facilities and complimentary expertise to develop Pomytkin's insights into research in many areas. Finland is logistically convenient to Russia as evidenced by the many wealthy Russians who have bought property there.

Shooting the messenger proved to be easier in my case than considering the science I was bringing. Getting funding for one of my companies was necessary to establish the credibility of my business model. I stopped speaking at venture fairs in Russia, tired of raising expectations there that Finland refused to help me fulfill.

***

Economic troubles in Finland and the rest of the EU have turned Finland's attention back in the direction of Russia. Nokia's sale to Microsoft was a highly visible sign of hard times ahead. Once synonymous with a resurgent Finnish innovation driven economy Nokia was replaced by Angry

Birds, a software company as the flagship Finnish technology in the international marketplace.

How about turning to Russia as an area of comparative advantage? I was making the argument that Finland had what Russia needed in 2007. Instead of funding Buddha Biopharma, a small start up promising to create a new industry, Tekes sent the largest amount of its funding to Nokia that year, and the next, and the next.

The conclusion I have been forced into is that the insular, small-minded Finns do not have what it takes to tap into the entrepreneurial parts of Russia that are destined to be the country's engines of growth and connection with the west. If it were possible to resurrect the "good old days" "public servants" in Helsinki and Moscow would be pleased. That relationship has experienced its own "near death experience".

With its reputation as a transparent, high tech country, trusted by the world community, Finland is in a position to provide potentially "transformational technologies" from Russia with the validation they need to attract western investors and industrial partners.

I conclude this chapter, which describes the conclusion of my relationship with Finland, with key portions of the report delivered by me to the government. As far as I can tell the report was delegated to an archive where it suffers a "near death experience", only to be revived here (and in its entirety in the appendix of "Bannana's Crime and Punishment").

Observations and Recommendations

Finland is in a position to provide mechanisms that are concrete and practical, and that recognize and address the unique circumstances and challenges of Russian sourced technology commercialization.

What are these unique Russian elements that must be addressed? The Russian business climate is opaque. There is a lack of trust among Russian innovators of their (Russian) internal structures.

Best evidence of this fact is the difficulty that Rusnano, the government designated commercialization mechanism, is having finding projects. President Medvedev has publicly expressed skepticism in Rusnano's ability to carry out its mission.

The "ownership" of Russian inventions is the subject of debate, controversy, and ongoing legislation. Historically, Institutes in Russia supported all research and development, much of it viewed in military or security terms. These Institutes have legitimate claims to participate and benefit from the commercialization of science in which they play a supporting role. The debate in Russia on how the interests of the Institutes and the individual inventors is balanced will continue. Much of this debate is internal (having to do with changes in legislation inside the Russian Federation) and fails to address the key issue of properly protecting Russian ideas, via patents, OUTSIDE of Russia.

As long as the Russian technology remains exclusively "inside" Russia, there will be concerns with respect to proper ownership of the technology, and the possibility that some future "claims" to the technology will surface that complicate, or nullify, agreements. The establishment of a company "outside" of Russia, with clean, clear rights to the technology outside of Russia, is a precondition to any licensing agreement with western partners.

This reality is recognized by Russians who have established companies outside of Russia. Many have left Russia permanently, contributing to a "brain drain". Given today's existing and emerging collaborative communication technologies, and the connectivity that exists to sites throughout Russia, a new paradigm is possible. Owners of Russian technology can remain in Russia, and build development teams in remote locations, that work in sync with foreign partners.

President Medvedev and many others have proclaimed the need for the Russian economy to diversify, a trend given additional importance by the current crisis. There has, in fact, been little progress in this regard. Finland is in a unique position (of competitive advantage) to provide what Russia needs. Innovation is fundamentally a bottom-up process, with ideas emerging from the minds of clever individuals. Russian industrial policy has traditionally been top down. Rusnano is an example.

It is unlikely that Russia will SUCCEED in the commercialization of its technologies in the western world ALONE. Western markets are sophisticated, with entrenched participants protective of their turf. Effective marketing and ongoing technical support networks make the entry of new players difficult. The barriers for entry are high for Russian technology, given its history of isolation and insulation from western markets.

Finland is in a privileged position to help, for reasons elaborated in the Russia Action Plan.

With its transparent business climate and trusted reputation for engineering prowess, Finland has rightfully focused on the merits of its "innovation engine" during its recent Presidency of the European Union. It is ironic that relatively little attention (so far) has been paid to the need to adapt and then apply this expertise to Finland's historical trading partner to the East.

The Russian Action Plan is a key step in this strategic direction. Finland is a small, well-connected country where questions are effectively routed to the place they can be addressed. So far, so good. But the fact is that Finland must make some changes if it is to address this opportunity successfully.

There is understandable suspicion, in Finland, of all things Russian. While reasonable, given history, this suspicion must be countered with a sincere open-mindedness about evaluating the promise and potential of Russian technology. It is quite possible that Russian technology can result in the rare "breakthroughs" that fuel technology transformations. Because of its long isolation, and its tradition of basic research in mathematics and the sciences, it is in fact probable that Russia represents the largest source of untapped (un-commercialized) ideas in the otherwise connected global village. Finland has a responsibility, and an obligation, to conduct an evaluation of Russian technology with this in mind.

It is necessary that this evaluation is conducted by persons specifically missioned with this responsibility, and equipped with the necessary skills (including speaking Russian). This mission should include "big thinking", the serious consideration that Russian technologies may represent transformational science. The first (and crucial!) step for such science is finding a commercially viable application area.

It is possible that the best commercial application of a technology is different from the one envisioned by the Russian owner of the technology. An understanding of the real needs of western industry is a key benefit that Finland can provide, in the initial assessment of any technology. This assessment should evaluate commercial success not only in Finland, but in the EU and the rest of the world.

VTT is in a position to play a key role in this initial assessment of Russian technology. VTT is also able to propose potential industrial partners as sponsors of VTT based projects. VTT is an ideal environment in which the Russian idea, once protected, can be developed into some prototype, making it understandable for Western investors or industrial partners.

VTT needs a "front end" mechanism, missioned with the task of routing a promising Russian technology to appropriate experts within its diverse organization, and delivering a prompt response that:
- identifies a promising application area or framework
- locates appropriate resources within VTT
- identifies potential partners for a VTT based project

Russian projects for this "front end" can come from various sources:
- the established Finnode network (St. Petersburg)
- an emerging Russian Venture Fair network (Moscow, St. Petersburg, Kazan, Novosibirsk, Rostov)
- word of mouth
- the Internet
- a book written by Mr. Vallila that describes the commercialization described herein.

It is crucial to build "success stories" that illustrate the business model described here. Russians have, over the years, been subjected to much information, and many promises, from both internal and external "experts". They are understandably skeptical about the viability of any scheme.

Only successful examples will convince potential participants to take the steps necessary to commercialize their inventions via Finland.

A crucial challenge for any owner of new technology is how to fund the initial steps of commercialization. Traditionally, such funding comes from the individuals themselves (often borrowing against their assets, such as their home) or from close friends or associates. Business angels have entered this space.

In Russia, funds such as Bortnik, are available for early stage technology. Such funds are internally focused. It is not very costly for a Russian to obtain a Russian patent. Much higher costs are associated with writing and filing a PCT patent application (which must be done within one year of the filing of a Russian patent) and obtaining subsequent international patent protection.

Before investing in such a process (filing a PCT application), the Russian inventor needs access to a trusted, reliable mechanism OUTSIDE of Russia able to provide a credible assessment of the commercial viability of a proposed technology. VTT has the expertise to provide this assessment. Currently, VTT lacks an effective "front end" missioned to examine and process Russian sourced technologies.

If a technology is found to have commercial potential, there is reason for the Russian owner to invest in its protection outside of Russia, via the PCT process. This should be done with the assistance of Intellectual Property (IP) specialists OUTSIDE of Russia. Finnish IP firms are in a strong position to provide this service.

Initial financial support for the technology must come from within Russia. It is not realistic to expect financial support from a foreign source, if the technology cannot attract Russian support. Once Russian support is demonstrated, then Finland, through Tekes, has the first opportunity to be the initial (privileged) foreign supporter.

Tekes support is limited to Finnish companies. This is as it should be. Access to Tekes support should, however, be made more understandable to those from outside Finland who take the steps to establish a company in Finland. The potential availability of support from TEKES (with no dilution of equity) is a strong incentive for a Russian inventor to consider establishing his foreign company in Finland.

The current Tekes application process is fundamentally flawed, if examined from the point of view of an applicant representing Russian technology. Most basically, the application must be filed in the Finnish language! This is an unnecessary barrier to effective communication. There is broad understanding of English in Finland (a tremendous advantage!) There is no reason to insulate the Tekes process from non-speakers of Finnish.

The benefits to Finland of being selected as the foreign home for a company founded on Russian based technology are numerous. If Finland is not capable of effectively addressing this opportunity, then Russian owners of promising technology will go elsewhere.

The establishment of a company OUTSIDE of Russia with clear and transparent ownership of international IP rights to the underlying technology is an essential element of the commercialization model described here. The commercialization of new technology involves many risks. The additional "business risk" associated with the ownership of any technology by an opaque Russian company makes its licensing to a western partner unlikely.

Finland is in a privileged position to fill this need. The Russia Action Plan states: "A challenge for Finland is to foster its expertise and services in order to create products that interest Russia".

Finland's existing commercialization engine can become such a product (actually a set of products and services). Today these products are not effectively presented. As explained above, proper representation requires a believable and trusted business model that credibly explains and supports the commercialization process from beginning to end, in English, and even in Russian. Only the existence of successful examples will make a model believable and inspire participation.

Once the Russian sourced technologies have been "incubated" in Finland, as described above, they can then be presented to the rest of the world, in order to attract additional investment or industrial partners in a position to distribute them globally. Finnish firms will, of course, have privileged access due to their proximity to the process. Elements of Finland's external commercialization mechanisms, such as Finnode offices in Silicon Valley and China, offer an excellent format for this broader distribution of technology.

Finland can brand itself as a world leader in the commercialization of Russian sourced technologies.

Rose, the pioneer

I conclude this book by returning to its source and inspiration, my mother Rose. When I saw Rose, in George Washington Hospital in her hospital bed, after driving to Washington DC from North Carolina upon hearing that she had suffered a heart attack, she greeted me with surprise, gratitude and had one wish:

"Please, give me a cigarette!"

A cigarette, in the recovery section of GW Hospital? Impossible! Absurd. A testimony to the grip this narcotic has on its victims. Rose told me how close to death she had come before being resuscitated by the rib breaking efforts that had brought her back.

"If that moment ever returns, I do not want to be brought back", she told me in no uncertain terms. Rose had seen a divine light, felt peace.

This instruction gave me comfort when, some weeks later, in North Carolina, I was faced with that choice. I had driven her to our home and placed her in a facility nearby where she was in the care of specialists. There Rose suffered another heart attack and was taken to the hospital.

I found her in a high tech monitoring station. The only sign of life was a signal on a green monitor that had peaks and valleys. I explained to the doctor what my mother had said to me and he ordered the disconnection of life support systems so that Rose could be more "comfortable". The line on the monitor went flat.

Do I wish Rose had lived long enough to see her grandchildren achieve what they have accomplished? Do I wish she were here to welcome the birth of great-grand children in Boston?

Of course.

Am I grateful for the candor of our lifelong exchanges, evidenced by the letters that constitute the body of this book, for giving me the guidance that I needed at the moment of decision on a "near death experience" for Rose?

Absolutely.

Rose was cremated holding three roses one for each of the three vagabonds who had arrived in New York in 1956. I buried some of her ashes in the back yard of the N Street house where Rose spent her last years watching the birds that would visit. Her happiest days there were babysitting Kristine and Sofia when we dropped them off, before they were old enough to join us on ski vacations.

Marja sculpted a piece that we affixed to the brick wall at the back of the yard above her final testing place. I took some of her ashes to San Francisco and threw them into the bay from the pier visible in the cover shot of this book. San Francisco was Rose's second choice as a place to plant Vallila roots in America but she felt it was too far away from Europe and chose Georgetown instead.

When Sofia and Chris decided to marry they chose the World War I memorial near Martin Luther King's statue in Washington as the location. DC made sense as a mid-point between North Carolina, from where many friends were coming, and Boston, their home.

Their choice was also a tribute to Rose. The day after the ceremony I visited the N Street house just down the street from Rose Park (given that name long before our Rose moved into the neighborhood). I said a prayer. I am sure that Rose is observing the progress of her progeny destined to make their mark in Boston, where the American story started.

This brave woman was the pioneer in the Vallila family who came to the new world so that her children, grandchildren and great-grandchildren could make their contribution to it.

Boston, my final resting place

In that Stanford speech in 2005 Steve Jobs spoke of the fact that dots can only be connected looking back.

Having travelled this journey so far I attempt to do this for the reader. My visit to China, anticipated in letters written in my early 20's, was accomplished in July 2000 when I flew from San Francisco to meet a delegation from Novosibirsk, Russia, in Beijing. That visit is described in "Bannana in Russia".

I did not imagine that I would get to China through Russia when in the Philippines. My Russian technology business development initiatives have brought me back to Asia, to Singapore, where I established Fuzzy Chip after being kicked out of Finland.

I am confident that Dr. Pomytkin's compound will achieve the recognition it deserves. How my support of his activities will ultimately be rewarded remained to be seen when I completed this book. I met lawyers in Boston who took an interest in my case. How it all ended is told in "Bannana in Boston", a book that awaits a final chapter (that will identify the investor who will make me rich) as I finished this one.

Some things I do know as I finish. I have survived numerous "near death experiences" and have found stability and peace in Boston. My monthly IBM checks pay the rent and social security feeds me while I wait for fortune of the financial kind to find me.

Having wandered much of the world I have ended up near my kids and their kids. Boston will be my final resting place.

***

What steps have I taken to minimize near death experiences? I have stayed away from cigarettes. It is the one piece of advice I force on anyone young I observe smoking that I consider worth saving. Popular culture seems to have moved in this direction after being the main reason the young started something on a whim that would overwhelm them.

I have stayed away from motorcycles. I have ridden some and experienced a thrill of acceleration and sense of freedom that I recognize has the potential to kill me, given my other tendencies.

I have stayed away from gun ownership. I have faith in my ability to talk my way out of any situation. It has worked so far. I admit to having second thoughts on this.

My sister Marja is alive, but has lost her ability to speak, no longer recognizes her daughter or me because of an advanced case of frontal lobe disorder. Would Pomytkin's compound have been of help if available? I doubt it. I know for sure how precious good health is.

Rose died at my age. Hemingway killed himself at 60. I prefer the Colonel Sanders trajectory. He found fortune late, when his secret formula for chicken was finally recognized.

ABOUT THE AUTHOR

Martti Vallila was born in Prague, Czechoslovakia, son of Olli, a Finnish diplomat (stationed there while negotiating post war reparations) and Czech mother, Rose. Martti immigrated to Washington DC at age seven with Rose and sister Marja, where he learned English (his fifth language) in public schools. He graduated from Stanford University in 1971 with a degree in anthropology and earned an MBA, with a concentration in international business, from the University of Chicago, in 1978. Martti lives in Boston. This is his fourth book.

Other Bannana Books:

Bannana in Russia
Bannana in the Legal Gulag
Bannana's Crime and Punishment
Bannana in Boston

Made in the USA
Charleston, SC
18 December 2015